S. Varnedoe
146 West 75th St., (#4B)
New York, N.Y. 10023
(212) 354-4916 or 799-9316

MARCEL DUCHAMP

MARCEL DUCHAMP.

by ALEXANDRIAN

CROWN PUBLISHERS, INC. - NEW YORK

Title page: MARCEL DUCHAMP
Photograph

Translated from the French by:
ALICE SACHS

Collection published under the direction of:
MADELEINE LEDIVELEC-GLOECKNER

Library of Congress Cataloging in Publication Data
Alexandrian, Sarane.
  Marcel Duchamp.

  Bibliography. p. 93
  1. Duchamp, Marcel, 1887–1968.
ND553.D774A7613   759.4   76–56831
ISBN 0–517–53008–2

PRINTED IN ITALY – © 1977 BY BONFINI PRESS CORPORATION, NAEFELS, SWITZERLAND
ALL RIGHTS OF REPRODUCTIONS BY A.D.A.G.P., PARIS
ALL RIGHTS IN THE U.S.A. ARE RESERVED BY CROWN PUBLISHERS, INC., NEW YORK, N.Y.

THE CHESS GAME, 1910   Oil on canvas, 44⅞″ × 57½″
Philadelphia Museum of Art, The Louise and Walter Arensberg Collection

For some people, Marcel Duchamp is the supreme master who rid painting of the need to express feeling or to obey any rigid aesthetic formula, a man who had assumed a completely new attitude toward both art and life; for others, impressed by the profound meaning of his work (and of his idleness), he is a sort of unconscious magician whose influence is enigmatic. Yet all opinions are in agreement in recognizing him as having an intellect which was exceptionally acute, powerfully logical even in its absurdities, which gave lasting brilliance to even the least of his creations. At each phase of his evolution, there were men ready to say of him, as did Pierre de

Massot in 1935: «Duchamp never stops thinking and, thinking, never stops creating. One can only remain overwhelmed by such intelligence. . . .» He was the only artist in the world who could reasonably be compared to a Zen or Taoist monk; one can admire him not only for what he created, but also for what he was, his life-style; he demonstrated a kind of detached attitude toward possible contingencies more effective than the passive resistance of a Buddhist. Duchamp was neither a painter, a sculptor, a poet, nor writer; he was *someone* rather than no one.

When one looks at photographs of Duchamp taken at different times, alone or in a group, in his youth or in his old age, what strikes one is the quality of his smile. It is obvious that this is the feature that is his most salient characteristic, to an extent not true of any other contemporary personality. Marcel Duchamp's smile epitomizes the *avant-garde* art of the twentieth century, as Voltaire's symbolized the activity of the Encyclopedists in the eighteenth century. But their thrust is different. Voltaire's smile was aggressive, sarcastic, and revealed the temperament of a man inclined to ridicule his enemies by inventing epigrams. Duchamp's smile is mocking and skeptical, expressing a serenity that comes with the refusal to conform and seeking less to offend than to question. It is not a smile that exposes the teeth, but a slight, almost imperceptible thinning of the lips; sometimes his mouth appears misleadingly serious, while he smiles out of the corner of his eye and his body assumes a position which denotes he is indulging in good-natured ridicule. One realizes that here is a master of irony, whose face, thoughtful and silent, seems to be saying to his interlocutor: «Are you sure?» Naturally, under these circumstances, no one can be sure of anything. To understand Duchamp one must analyze what is hidden behind his smile and how he succeeded in using it to fascinate successive generations of innovators.

Marcel Duchamp was born July 28, 1887, in Blainville, Normandy, the third son of the notary Justin-Isidore Duchamp, and grew up in a milieu receptive to painting, music and the game of chess. At a young age, he could contemplate on the walls of his parents' villa the paintings and etchings of his grandfather, Emile Nicolle (died in 1896), a former ship broker who became a professional painter. The Duchamp family consisted of three boys — Gaston, Raymond and Marcel — and three girls — Suzanne, Yvonne and Magdeleine — which explains why later he ascribed a symbolic significance to the number three. Four of the children displayed artistic talent early on. The eldest, Gaston, who started out as a notary's clerk in Rouen, decided to become a painter and at the age of twenty left for Paris to serve his apprenticeship in the Cormon studio. His father requesting that he use a pseudonym, he chose the name of Jacques Villon as a tribute to his favorite poet, François Villon. Raymond began medical studies which he gave up in 1898, at the age of twenty-two, in order to devote his time to sculpture under the name of Duchamp-Villon. As to Suzanne Duchamp, two years younger than Marcel, according to those close to her, she was «born with a crayon in her hand.» While still very small, as soon as a meal was over she enthusiastically started to sketch the portraits of all those around the table. M. Duchamp gave benign encouragement to his artistic progeny, regularly doling out sums which he deducted from their shares of his inheritance so that each would be treated altogether fairly.

Duchamp's interest in painting was not really awakened until he became a student in the Bossuet School in Rouen. Two of his fellow students painted, and he carried on long discussions with them on Impressionism, which was still generally disparaged and with which they were familiar only through reproductions in books. In 1902 he essayed his first canvases, *Church at Blainville* and *Landscape at Blainville* (see p. 9), using the technique of Monet which he had learned through reading about it: developing his theme in the open air, employing pure colors and stippling his canvas, seeking always to produce the effect of diffused light. If these paintings had been done by some other novice of the period, it would be enough to state that they indicated a

*Man Wearing a
Top Hat, 1909
a ink and pencil on
aper, 12⅜" × 7¾"
Collection:
er & Ekstrom, Inc.,
New York*

remarkable talent for a lad of fifteen; certain of Monet's imitators, such as Loiseau, did not do any better. However, these efforts should not be judged by the ordinary criteria of the art connoisseur, for they are the first expressions of a question which obsessed Duchamp from early adolescence and which he constantly attempted to resolve by a succession of varied experiments: *What is painting?*

He was already convinced that he knew what Impressionism was; in order to be counted as one of its practitioners, he had only to continue to paint impressionist works until he had evolved his personal style. But Duchamp was not one to repeat himself. He felt that his search for the ultimate meaning and potentialities of painting could not be successful unless he refused to belong to a single school, no matter how original it might be. The following year he limited himself to drawing, while he reflected on possible ways of going beyond Impressionism. He thought he could escape from its influence with his *Portrait of Marcel Lefrançois* (1904), in which, using as a model the nephew of his maid, Clémence, he experimented with a process utilized by the painters of the Renaissance: he first painted the portrait in black and white and, when it was dry, applied transparent colors in a wash, then varnished it.

After obtaining his baccalaureate, Duchamp went to Paris on October 1904 to join his brother, Jacques Villon, who was living on the Butte Montmartre at 71 rue Caulaincourt. At this time Villon was specializing in color engraving and humorous drawings and was on the staff of the *French Courier,* an illustrated weekly founded by Forain. Thanks to his brother, Duchamp became acquainted with the best caricaturists of Montmartre, including Léandre, whose satire was directed against the mores of the «human menagerie,» and Willette, at the other end of the scale, a happy and fanciful soul who, when his drawings of Pierrots and Pierrettes were compared to the art of Watteau, declared he was prouder of founding the Montmartre fire brigade. In this bohemian and free-thinking circle, Duchamp's humor grew more robust and he was stamped with the imprint of the Parisian spirit, based on keen observation of the absurdities of the world and distinguished by its biting wit, its attacks against sham and its risqué allusions.

In principle, Duchamp was in Paris to perfect his painting, and therefore was supposed to take some courses at the Julian Academy, where members of the Institute prepared pupils for the entrance examination to the School of Beaux-Arts. But he found this academic instruction so distasteful that he preferred to spend his time playing pool in the cafés of Montmartre or sketching passers-by when they were unaware of it. At the same time, his immediate plans for the future were threatened by two years' mandatory military service. In order to take advantage of a law which was about to be repealed and which permitted qualified artisans to serve for just one year, he returned to Rouen in July 1905 and spent a training period with a printer of engravings; this enabled him to show a few proofs of engravings which he had produced to the officers, enlist in the army as an «art worker,» and be excused from the second year of duty.

In October 1906, once again a civilian, Marcel Duchamp came back to Paris and again settled at number 65, then at number 73 rue Caulaincourt. That same year Jacques Villon had left the Butte Montmartre to take up residence in a villa in Puteaux; thus the younger brother could see his sibling only on Sundays. Duchamp lived alone in Montmartre for almost two years; he may have been meeting persons who influenced his career, but their names are not known to us. Once again he took up his studies at the Julian Academy and decided to try to gain admission to the School of Beaux-Arts. The first test called for a charcoal study of a nude; the one he did caused him to be rejected. This failure was certainly a blow to his pride and led him to concentrate on the study of nudes for several years. It is therefore not surprising that in his drawings and paintings there are nude women in all sorts of positions: at the top of a ladder, in a tub, pulling

LANDSCAPE AT BLAINVILLE, 1902   Oil on canvas, 24″ × 19¹¹/₁₆″   Collection: Vera and Arturo Schwarz, Milan

On the Cliff, 1905 Oil on canvas, 21⅞″ × 15⅛″
Collection: Mary Sisler, Xavier Fourcade, Inc., New York

MAN SEATED BY A WINDOW, 1907 Oil on canvas, 21⅞″ × 15¼″
Collection: Mary Sisler, Xavier Fourcade, Inc., New York

RED HOUSE AMONG APPLE TREES, 1908   Oil on canvas, 21⁵/₈″ × 16¹⁵/₁₆″
Collection: Galleria Schwarz, Milan

on black stockings, etc. It is as if he wished to prove to an imagined critic — in reality his former examiner — that there could be many unconventional ways of treating nudes. Seemingly insignificant factors such as this should not be overlooked in analyzing the psychology of an artist, for many works are inspired by the desire to get revenge for a slight or an adverse criticism.

Without losing sight of his eternal question: « What is painting? » Duchamp completed a series of caricatures for the *French Courier* and for *Laugh* between 1907 and 1910 (see pp. 34–35). It would be a great mistake to underestimate this phase of his career and to conclude that he did these drawings merely to earn money. Jacques Villon and Marcoussis (who signed as Markous at the time) made a good living as caricaturists because they sold many full-page drawings, often in color. Duchamp, on the other hand, produced thirty at the most in three years, always in line, and those in *Laugh* were quarter-page size; therefore he depended more on his father's money than on the profits from his output. It is obvious that his impetus was the amusement he derived from exercises that permitted him to evaluate the elements of humorous drawings.

It should be noted moreover, that it was only at the beginning of the twentieth century in France that people began to analyze the concept of humor; it was the subject of a course given by Fernand Baldensperger, lecturer in Nancy, in 1900. He expressed regret that the term was used only to describe literature and not painting, and was grateful that humorists had « the heroism to refuse to be like everyone else and succeeded, sometimes to excess, in protecting their innermost selves from banality and debasement.» Caricaturists, formerly called satirists or parodists, would henceforth lay claim to the title of humorists. The Society of Cartoonists, founded in 1904, had its first Salon in April 1911 at the Fashion Palace (Jacques Villon, a member of the committee, showed six watercolors and one engraving) and its president, Louis Morin, wrote in the catalogue: « With a subtle pursing of the lips, a slight wink, humor is the last display of joyfulness which we are permitted.» Thus, in his drawing, Duchamp tried to define the new concept of graphic humor. If the caricatures of Villon and Marcoussis were a form of social criticism, those of Duchamp provoked laughter by depicting scenes from private life. His style was elegant, perhaps even overly refined, playing on the contrast between the demeanor of people and what they said. The caption was frequently based on a pun, a semantic ambiguity or an erotic innuendo. In *Purée,* he invented the following dialogue between a kept woman and her lover: « Do you want half of what my *Viennese* gives me? » — « That's a *tart* I don't eat.» In *Objects and Pawnshop,* a couple discussed what they were going to leave « at my aunt's,» that is to say at the pawnbroker's. The wife protested: « O no! Jules. Not Mother's watch! » « Why not? It will still be in the family.» In his composition, Duchamp clearly applied the lessons learned from Jacques Villon, who could suggest movement by an « evocative line.» He drew gestures with a pretty inventiveness, as when he placed a violinist in front of a female customer (*The Maestro and His Works*) or made people aware of the hesitation of a young man who, while helping his girl friend to remove her jacket, reflected sheepishly: « I'm afraid I'll never know just when one should embrace women » (*Three Legs*). Duchamp's caricatures should be carefully observed; it is through them that he began to sharpen the claws of his irony for the world to see.

Yet he continued to seek a way to go beyond Impressionism in painting. He turned to the « Nabi » painters and especially those known as « Intimists » or painters of family life. During a vacation in Yport in 1907, he painted *On the Cliff* (see p. 10) in order to demonstrate how to paint a seascape, and *Man Seated by a Window* (see p. 11), which depicts the actor Félix Barré, a friend of the family, in a classical pose of the Intimists: a figure or a still life before a window opening onto a landscape — a device Bonnard adopted to portray an interior in its relation to the exterior. Other portraits by Duchamp, such as those of his sister Yvonne (see p. 22), of a son of the Candel family (see p. 23) and of the maid Clémence (see p. 21) indicate that he preferred to depict an intimate scene in a closed milieu and to focus attention on the person.

In July 1908, Duchamp left Montmartre and moved to Neuilly, where he spent the next five years on the Avenue Amiral-Joinville. Thus he was able to see his two brothers, domiciled in a park in Puteaux, more frequently, and intensify his research. He had discovered Matisse's paintings at the Autumn Salon and as a result felt a desire to experiment with the style of the Fauve school. With *Red House among Apple Trees* (see p. 12) (the house was that of Kupka, Jacques Villon's neighbor in Puteaux) and *Peonies in a Vase* he took his first steps in the use of strident colors, still impelled by the same concern for methodical and thoughtful exploration of new techniques, a continued quest for the meaning of painting. In 1909, it would appear that Duchamp definitely resolved to make painting his career; he entered competitions, showed two paintings at the Salon of Independents and, a few months later, three others, among them *On the Cliff*, at the Autumn Salon. He decided that he was ready to face the public with an artistic output which took into account the trends of the time.

Throughout 1910, Duchamp's work underwent the double influence of Fauvism and Intimism. In this spirit he painted in Rouen, where he always went for Christmas, *Nude Seated in a Tub, Nude with Black Stockings* and, following his return to Neuilly, *Two Nudes* (see p. 32) and *Red Nude* (see p. 30). Duchamp still was under the influence of Matisse, whose retrospective exhibition that year at the Bernheim Junior Gallery he admired, as shown in *The Artist's Father* (see p. 24) or in *Nana*, the sketch of a brunette in a bright green blouse. One innovation should be noted: for the first time, he introduced humor into his painting, without resorting to caricature and while respecting accepted artistic standards. As an example, *Laundry Barge* (see p. 29) is a very subtle joke; from the title one is led to expect a reproduction of the group of studios on the rue Ravignan which Max Jacob had baptized the Laundry Barge, and where Picasso, Juan Gris, Van Dongen and others resided. In reality, Duchamp depicted a barge moored at the bridge of Neuilly, where each day he saw laundresses performing their chores; a true laundry barge, on which laundry was drying, was in his mind the counterpart of the imitation Laundry Barge of the Montmartre painters, in which canvases were drying. In the *Portrait of Doctor Dumouchel* (see p. 37) he obtained a humorous effect by the extreme color contrast (red and green) and the ambiguous pose of the subject, who appears to applaud or to strike cymbals without one being able to see his second hand. Lastly, he expanded his artistic range by implementing the lesson learned from Cézanne. He had seen paintings by Cézanne at the Vollard Gallery and was inspired by them to execute *The Chess Game* (see p. 5), in which he showed his two brothers competing against each other in chess in their garden in Puteaux, while their wives are taking tea alongside them. *The Chess Game,* exhibited in the Autumn Salon of 1910, earned him the title of full member, which enabled him henceforth to show his paintings without their first being approved by the selection committee. Several of the exhibitors were eager to make his acquaintance, and he was able to shake the hand of the *enfant terrible* of the Autumn Salon, Francis Picabia, which marked the beginning of a lasting association.

Having replaced the influence of Matisse with that of Cézanne, he refused to be completely dominated by this new master. Duchamp's aim was not to be a first-class practitioner of the latest and best artistic trend, but to explore everything that could be done in painting. At that moment there were still fanatic adherents of allegorical art, which sprang from the synthetic bent of the Pont-Aven school. One of Duchamp's friends, Pierre Girieud, was a convinced disciple of this movement, and Duchamp decided to try it in his turn. He started with *Paradise,* an idyllic vision of innocence whose sacerdotal connotations are not lacking in humor, in view of the posture of

14

COACHMAN ON BOX,
1904–05
Pencil and watercolor,
8¼″ × 5⅛″
Collection: Vera and
Arturo Schwarz, Milan

15

*Suzanne Duchamp Seated, 1903–1905   Drawing in color pencils, 19½″ × 12⅝″
Collection: Madame Marcel Duchamp, Villiers-sous-Grez*

Doctor Dumouchel who served as the model for Adam. One can reasonably conclude that Duchamp, while depicting an allegory, was making fun of it and actually tending to parody it. *The Bush* (see p. 31) competed with *The Three Graces* which Girieud destined for the Independents. Two nude women — one brunette, standing, her hand resting on the head of the other one; the second blonde, kneeling — are posed before a blue bush: a double apparition, enticing and haunting, threatening to make Duchamp break his vows of celibacy. A principal subject of allegories ever since the Middle Ages had been the Temptation of Saint Anthony, in which were unfolded the incidents that troubled the meditations of the anchorite. *The Bush* represented the Temptation of Saint Marcellus. In *Baptism* two more women, with still more voluptuous figures, represent this same carnal temptation. In *The Breeze on the Japanese Apple Tree,* he availed himself of an exotic style to describe how best to resist turbulent passions: a Buddhist ascetic squats impassibly before a scrubby tree ruffled by the wind, that is to say by the breath of desire. But here again we have pictorial trickery, a painting whose surface esoteric quality conceals a lively mischievousness; for Duchamp patterned his wise man on the « Japanese Woman » who also acted as a model for his brothers, and who posed for his own watercolor, *Dark Skin* (see p. 27).

This allegorical style, half serious, half ironical, reaches its culmination in *Young Man and Girl in Spring* (see p. 40), dedicated to his sister Suzanne who had just married a druggist. Marcel perceived Suzanne as his female counterpart; she was approximately the same age and, after leaving the School of Beaux-Arts in Rouen, had made her debut as a professional artist by exhibiting a portrait of Jacques Villon before his easel at the Salon of Norman Artists in 1910. Duchamp wished solemnly to spell out what united them and what separated them. The young man and the young girl, in an identical transport of joy, raise their arms toward the branches of a tree from which hangs a sort of huge translucent apple. This is what unites them: a common ambition to taste of the fruit of the tree of knowledge, that is to say to learn to understand the world through painting (the apple symbolized the globe of the earth, seen as transparent). But at the base of the tree there is a V angle, whose two vectors seem to be pushing the two bodies away from each other. This is what separates them: the difference between their sexes and its various emotional implications. Suzanne has married, while Marcel intends to remain a bachelor; if they are nude as they reach out toward the tree which represents paradise, it is because they seek to enter the realm of knowledge without prejudice, not because they are parading a nuptial union.

*   *   *

From the moment it opened on March 25, the Salon of Independents of 1911 was the scene of a revolution. Room 41, in which were grouped the exhibitors who, in a reaction against Fauvism, were producing paintings in which geometric forms and muted tones predominated, was invaded by an indignant horde. Apollinaire loudly proclaimed that these innovators should be christened Cubists, a title intended to ridicule them. Duchamp had not waited for this event to become interested in the budding cubist movement: he had seen paintings by Picasso and Braque in the Kahnweiler Gallery and had preferred the approach of Braque, whom he subsequently visited in his studio.

Duchamp became an adherent of Cubism only in order to contribute to it one thing which was lacking: movement. The defenders of the school were embarrassed and reluctantly acknowledged his innovations; Apollinaire was content to state absurdly that he was attempting to reconcile art and people. As the movement waned, it became apparent that Duchamp was the only one of the group to advance *subjective Cubism.* The aim of the Cubists was to analyze objects by showing all the sides at once on a single canvas, using the technique of a « flattening of planes. » When they painted an individual, they depicted all the facets, in order to establish a system of volumetric relationships. Duchamp did not choose to superimpose the various views of an object, as if they could be seen simultaneously, in order to show all its global ramifications; he used the methods advocated by the Cubists to externalize what he felt when faced with the reality of his personal life. In doing this, he stripped his work of any suspicion of lyricism or tenderness; he painted emotion objectively, in coldly analytical fashion, as if he were doing a still life.

Thus, in *Sonata* (see p. 39) he utilized the cubist palette to depict the female contingent of the Duchamp family. Yvonne is playing the piano, Magdeleine the violin, and Suzanne listens to them pensively, occupying all of the foreground. The mother (whose face is seen at the same time in profile and full-face) stands in the center of the picture; she thus provides the scene with symmetry and rhythm, like a metronome or a crossbeam of scales. It is apparent that Duchamp, through the medium of an effective motif, wanted to achieve the equivalent of the four sides of an object; in this instance the three girls are the three sides which complement the portrait of the mother, and the group is so positioned that it is diamond-shaped.

Dulcinea (see p. 47) is another striking example of subjective Cubism. It is the portrait of a young woman whom Duchamp saw walking her dog on a path in Neuilly every day; he was somewhat smitten but did not dare speak to her, and she never paid any attention to him. He shows her five times in his painting, going in five different directions; three times she is clothed, twice she is nude, but she always wears the same hat. He was not painting the woman as she actually was, but as he imagined her to be and as he desired her. He does not sublimate; on the contrary, it is as though he were denigrating her in order to combat the attraction which she had for him. He disrobes her with his eyes and renders his judgment on her physical attributes by removing all those coverings that concealed and disguised them, leaving only the hat as a symbol of her femininity.

With *Yvonne and Magdeleine (Torn) in Tatters* (see p. 46) he introduced the notion of time into painting. Yvonne and Magdeleine are four profiles floating in space, but these profiles are grouped in such a way as to distinguish what they are at the present moment, while still adolescent, from what they will become later. Thus two delicate countenances provide a sharp contrast to two masks distorted by old age. Nothing similar can be found in any other cubist painting; when other Cubists showed several aspects of a person, is was not to depict what he or she was at different stages of life, but simply to express variations in volume.

The three Duchamp brothers assumed such importance in the cubist movement that the name, « Puteaux Group, » was used to describe the painters who assembled on Sundays at Jacques Villon's and who advocated a scientific Cubism which differed from the intuitive Cubism of Picasso and Braque. The Puteaux Group, consisting of Jean Metzinger, Albert Gleizes, Fernand Léger, Roger de la Fresnaye, the decorator André Mare and a number of others, discussed the « fourth dimension » and the Section of Gold, with intervals of relaxation for activities such as archery. Most of the Cubists relied on mathematics and physics without the slightest understanding of them; an insurance agent, Maurice Princet, whom they took to be an undiscovered genius, gave them popular explanations of outer space. At Puteaux, the artists desired greater precision; Marcel Duchamp, who had read the *Elementary Treatise on Four-Dimensional Geometry* by Esprit Jouffret (1903), spoke as an expert on dimensions, the field of the fourth degree, in which curved spaces circumscribed hypervolume.

In order to honor the lucidity and «synthetic thought processes» extolled by his two brothers, Duchamp resolved to paint them playing chess and to give objective form to their mental tension and not only to their physical attitudes. After several studies in ink and watercolor, he showed them in a first picture confronting each other feverishly, with the pieces of the chessboard dancing a saraband around them (*Portrait of Chess Players*; see back cover). The picture gives concrete form to their mental exertions as they concentrate on their next moves; this is why their silhouettes are of a ghostly vagueness and the intensity of their thought processes have almost eradicated any individual peculiarities. In the final version, each of the players is cut in two, which indicates what his intentions are and also that, as he projects what his opponent is going to do, he is at once himself and the other man (*The Chess Players,* see p. 45). Duchamp painted this second picture in the light of an incandescent burner, having determined that gas casts a greenish light. He subsequently explained: «When you paint under a green light and the next day look at the work in daylight, it is much more mauve, much grayer, like the tones the Cubists used at that period. It was an easy method of achieving a blurring and a grayish dullness of tone.»

Duchamp read a great deal; on discovering Jules Laforgue, for whom he felt an affinity because of the bantering manner and ingenious semantic inventiveness of this poet, he drew for his own pleasure about ten illustrations of Laforgue's poems, which he interpreted freely. For example, his graphic extension of *Once More to This Star,* whose verses ranted against the sun because of its spots, was a sketch of a man's head between two nudes, one facing front, the other seen from the back ascending a staircase, as if what Laforgue had said about the sun could also apply to women. He was also interested in the works of E.-J. Marey on color photography, as it was discussed in his book, *Movement* (1894), and was undoubtedly struck by the «geometric photograms,» schemas of the course which Marey successfully followed in photographing an individual dressed in black, whose arms and legs were marked by white lines which alone were visible on the picture. Duchamp foresaw the possibility of expressing movement not as the eye was capable of seizing it, but by depicting each of its successive stages from the beginning to the end of its trajectory. He was eager to do better than Kupka, painting in *Planes in Color* (1911) the movement of a woman turning around to look behind her.

When, in November 1911, Raymond Duchamp-Villon asked six friends from the Puteaux Group to decorate his kitchen, Duchamp gave him as his contribution a small picture featuring a coffee mill, seen from above and from the side, dissected as it crushed beans, a dotted line and an arrow indicating the rotary motion of the wrist. Duchamp was very proud of the arrow, which, as a matter of fact, preceded everything that would be done subsequently by the Bauhaus to express direction, speed and momentum. His *Coffee Mill,* said Breton, «alongside the guitars of the Cubists takes on the aspect of an infernal machine»; it is one of the first examples of «mechanical painting,» with which even Léger was not yet concerned.

The *Coffee Mill* (see p. 48) was an example of kinetic Cubism, which succeeded the subjective Cubism of earlier experiments. It remained for Duchamp to reconcile the two, which he did in December in *Sad Young Man in a Train* (see p. 56), for which he conceived the idea during a trip from Paris to Rouen. The young man, standing in the corridor, is shaken by the jolting of the train; as it is affected by these vibrations, his body is in effect broken up into oscillating lines. Although the brown tones and the black border suggest melancholy and the subject's pipe seems to confess it is a self-portrait, the title aimed to provoke public controversy rather than to denote Duchamp's state of mind at that particular time.

It was logical that all of his inventions made use of Duchamp's preferred subject, the nude. For instance, he eventually conceived of a nude in movement, transformed into a sort of ambulatory machine, and placed it in a particularly incongruous, antiacademic position: descending a staircase. What gave him the idea for such a creation? Perhaps his two drawings of nudes on a ladder in 1907; seeing the woman who was posing for him descend the ladder where she had been perched, he may have observed that this pose was a more unusual one to reproduce than a classic position. He completed two versions of the *Nude Descending a Staircase* (see p. 55), emphasizing the offensive thrust of the body, which was truly a projectile hurled toward the spectator. The first version, in December 1911, has the staircase appearing in back of the nude, in an area marked off by a painted border. In the second, larger in size, the anatomical machinery of the woman occupies the total surface of the picture; flesh tones are replaced by the colors of wood; the title, inscribed in capital letters, establishes a relation between written language and the shocking effect of the image.

This painting was such a revolutionary departure from even the most advanced experiments of the *avant-garde* that, when he wished to exhibit it at the Salon of Independents in March 1912, Gleizes and Le Fauconnier requested that he withdraw it, in order not to distort the concept of Cubism as they understood it. Duchamp took back his painting, dismayed to discover to what extent conformity was demanded even in a school which purportedly was fighting tradition. Where, then, was freedom in art? Pierre Dumont, reviewing the salon in *Men of the Day,* deplored his exclusion. «Marcel Duchamp is showing only one drawing. This is regrettable, for it does not permit us to appreciate fully this artist's unusual talents.» In no way discouraged, Duchamp continued his efforts to unify and strengthen the movement, persisting all the more because he was convinced by the exhibition of Futurists at the Bernheim Junior Gallery in February 1912 that he was doing something different. On meeting Boccioni, he had concluded that he was taking another road than Boccioni's dynamism. The Futurists of the period had renounced the painting of nudes, while he was desirous of using the nude as a symbol of speed.

Thus he drew *Two Nudes: One Strong and One Swift,* in which the strong nude was portrayed by vertical lines, while the swift nude dissolved in shifting perspectives. In April, the drawing, *The King and Queen Traversed by Swift Nudes* and the watercolor, *The King and Queen Traversed by Nudes at High Speed* (see p. 50) expressed, with subtle differences, the notion that bodies in movement could be represented by strokes tracing a direction. Two stable blocks of volume are shaken in the wake of these running nudes. In the following month, his experiments culminated in a large painting, *The King and Queen Surrounded by Swift Nudes,* (see front cover) which in one perfect unity combined allegory with «the static representation of movement.» The king and the queen, inspired by chess pieces, symbolized Duchamp's father and mother; between them, like a waterfall going back to its source, a swift stream flowing backwards, their children burst forth like an eager current rushing toward an unknown destination. Duchamp thereby materialized his concept of the family by showing that the father and the mother are solid and enduring, whereas the children are the fluid, changing elements, tenuously linked together by their course toward the future.

At that time an important event stimulated him to take a new path and to pass from one phase of artistic experimentation to a phase of untrammeled inventiveness: a spectacle produced by Firmin Gémier at the Antoine Theatre, *Impressions of Africa* by Raymond Roussel, which he attended in May 1912 in the company of Apollinaire, Picabia and Gabrielle Buffet. In order to appreciate fully what influence Roussel exerted on Duchamp, one must be aware that he had not read the novel, *Impressions of Africa,* published by Lemerre in October 1909; he fell under the spell of this bizarre world through the play in four acts which the author had adapted from his book, and which featured great numbers of extras in costume, many acrobats and music. This point is important, for if Duchamp had been inspired by Roussel's novel, he could properly be

Clémence, 1910   Oil on canvas, 24″ × 19⅞″   Collection: Ekstrom & Cordier, Inc., New York

PORTRAIT OF YVONNE DUCHAMP, 1909   Oil on canvas, $34^{1}/_{16}'' \times 26^{1}/_{2}''$
Collection: Mary Sisler, Xavier Fourcade, Inc., New York

PORTRAIT OF YOUNG BOY OF CANDEL FAMILY, 1908   Oil on canvas, $27^{15}/_{16} \times 22^{5}/_{8}''$
Collection: Mary Sisler, Xavier Fourcade, Inc., New York

PORTRAIT OF THE ARTIST'S FATHER, 1910   Oil on canvas, 36¼″ × 28¾″
Philadelphia Museum of Art, The Louise and Walter Arensberg Collection

accused of creating a «literary» painting. In the theatre he saw, independent of any work of literature, only a series of animated tableaux which struck him as consistent with the goal he himself pursued in painting movement. In addition, the story that unfolded before his eyes was in part a parable, which illuminated the meaning of what he had confusedly been seeking. One can understand the nature of the revelation Duchamp had that evening, only if one knows under what conditions the drama was played and the story it told.

Publicized throughout Paris by posters illustrating the principal scenes, between May 11 and June 10 *Impressions of Africa* caused the greatest sensation of any production since *King Ubu*. The spectators sneered, hissed, screamed and interrupted the actors by throwing pennies at them; Duchamp and his friends, in the midst of a tumultuous crowd who protested against the drama as an insult to common sense, saw in it the manifestation of a new genius. In the first act, the passengers on the steamship *Lyncée,* grounded in a region of equatorial Africa, are the captives of Talou VII, king of Ponukélé, and have to wait two months for their ransom to be paid. The historian Julliard says to his companions: «My friends, for two months we will have to struggle against a terrible enemy, boredom, which in this part of the world is a real curse for white men and can lead to the worst kind of catastrophes, to sickness, to bloody quarrels; at any price, it is essential to be constantly diverted. To this end, I propose that you establish a peculiar club, where each member will be obliged to distinguish himself by an *original work.*» All of these works were to be presented at the Gala of the Incomparables, on the Square of the Trophies in Ejur, capital of Ponukélé. Each person, filled with competitive spirit, got ready. The chemist Bix, thanks to the ability to dilate of the metal *bexium,* which he discovered, constructed a «thermodynamic orchestra» enclosed in a mobile cage; the student Louise Montalescot, whose lungs were metallic tubes, built a «painting machine»; among the other inventions of the competitors were an earthworm playing a zither, a wind-propelled clock from Never-Never Land, a statue of whalebone rolling on tracks made of calf's lungs. As for Julliard, named president of the Incomparables Club, he created the award to be given for the most meritorious entries. «I have found an insignia which is both unusual and simple to reproduce. I have selected the fourth letter of the Greek alphabet, the capital Delta which has the form of a triangle. There will be six, each with a ring on top, and hung on a piece of blue ribbon.» (Similarly, in 1921 Duchamp proposed the creation of a Dadaist insignia made of «4 letters, DADA, in metal separated and linked by a thin chain.»)

It is easy to imagine the mental ferment this spectacle produced. He was enchanted by this fable, which sought to demonstrate that the creative individuals in a society, banded together, tended to form a league to oppose intellectual sterility. He resolved to dedicate himself to a spectacular work which would make him worthy of membership in the Incomparables' Club. This work would parody scientific activity, retaining only its respect for research, regardless of whether or not it served a useful purpose. Duchamp became persuaded that the concept of creativity, supposedly nourished by inspiration, had to be replaced, in art as in literature, by the concept of originality and inventiveness. Roussel appeared to him to be a master of inventiveness, since he invented inventors, and all of the ingenious devices dreamed up by his characters were really his own. At the same time, Duchamp recognized the effect produced by a writer who described an invention: he was the butt of general hilarity. The man who would paint something inventive — and Duchamp was now ambitious to be that man — had to expect an outburst of laughter. The best thing was to foresee this, to anticipate the probable reaction, indeed even to try to bring it about. It was in this spirit that, after seeing *Impressions of Africa,* Duchamp decided to paint a «hilarious picture.»

NUDE STANDING, 1910
Gouache on cardboard,
$23^5/_8'' \times 14^{15}/_{16}''$
Rouen Museum

NUDE WITH DARK SKIN, 1910 Watercolor on paper, 18″ × 18″
Philadelphia Museum of Art, The Louise and Walter Arensberg Collection

What would the motif be? On this point, Duchamp had no hesitation. «Love, a veritable storehouse of the comical never adequately exploited,» according to Baudelaire, who advised that this comic genre be expressed by stressing the disparity between the subject and the tone; for example, describing a couple of lovers by depicting them as «amorous insects.» A mind as keen as Duchamp's could not be satisfied with such a facile solution; he would portray love as a mechanism whose every cog contributed to a motion which was foreseeable and lacking in mystery. By studying men and women in the climactic moments of their intimacy as if they were machines carrying out precise functions, he would obtain an effect of glacial irony. In July 1912, he executed a large drawing showing three anthropomorphic figures in which the center one is apparently being attacked by the other two; the title: *First sketch of: The Bride Stripped Bare by her Bachelors,* with this comment in pencil: *Mechanism of modesty — mechanical modesty* (see p. 52). The same month, during a visit to Munich, he did a drawing and a watercolor of a mechanomorphic *Virgin,* and he began two oil paintings which he would finish in August: *Passage from the Virgin to the Bride* (see p. 53), a collection of cranks, pistons and gears whose operation is suggested by discrete dotted lines; and *Bride* (see p. 54), an apparatus at rest. He abandoned the use of the brush to crush and spread the paste with his fingers, in a resolve to be liberated from all convention. These were the preliminary studies for the «hilarious picture» which would reveal at the same time the depths of love and the depths of art.

People have wondered why Duchamp was so violently opposed to marriage, treating it like a hit-the-baby game at a country fair. Arturo Schwarz has argued that *The Bride Stripped Bare* is the result of an «unconscious incestuous love» which Duchamp felt for his sister Suzanne, whose marriage the year before had wounded him deeply. According to this theory, his frustration caused him to feel resentment against all women and in addition to write on the back of the painting *Apropos of Little Sister* (see p. 38), depicting the last-born child, Magdeleine: «A Study of Woman / Shit.» But a more orthodox psychoanalytical interpretation would be that this prejudice was based on Duchamp's relationship with his mother, whose indifference he resented. It is still more probable that he was trying to give a philosophical justification of the fact that he was unmarried, unlike his brothers. He reflected on the nature of marriage in such a manner that the single state seemed preferable to him. One is reminded of the reminiscences of Jules Laforgue, who ended his poem, *Celibacy, celibacy, there is nothing but celibacy,* with these verses: «Human history: history of *one* bachelor,» and who, in his *Complaint of Celibate Twilights,* wailed: «I am so wearied of art! / Repeating myself, how my head aches!...» Laforgue, in his notes *On Woman,* wondered what virginity really meant to the female sex. «That enormous, revolutionary step, to wit, / no longer to be a virgin! Does that change them? No! Look at them in the streets. Which are untouched and which ones wounded? Their eyes, their mien are the same.» Duchamp, in *The Bride Stripped Bare,* was trying to find out in what way a man, as well as a woman, was transformed qualitatively by the act of passing from virginal innocence to carnal knowledge and to analyze all the consequences of this act.

According to the *Gil Blas* of September 2, 1912, Marcel Duchamp intended to send to the next Autumn Salon a painting called *Section of Gold;* perhaps he first chose this title in an effort to define conjugal harmony in mathematical terms. At the end of the month, he took an automobile trip to Etival, in the Jura, with Picabia, Gabrielle Buffet and Apollinaire; in the course of the excursion they exchanged the most extraordinary ideas on how best to emancipate Cubism. They went over the details of the Salon of the Section of Gold, which was held in October in the quarters of a furniture dealer on the rue La Boétie; and Duchamp was inspired to write a text about a hilarious canvas, which imitated a wood surface (pine or polished mahogany), and had «the machine with

LAUNDRY BARGE, 1910   Oil on canvas, 26″ × 29⅛″
Collection: Mary Sisler, Xavier Fourcade, Inc., New York

RED NUDE, 1910   Oil on canvas, 36¼″ × 28¾″
National Gallery of Canada, Ottawa

THE BUSH, 1910–1911   Oil on canvas, 50″ × 36¼″
Philadelphia Museum of Art, The Louise and Walter Arensberg Collection

Two Nudes, 1910   Oil on canvas, 39″ × 31¹¹/₁₆″   Collection: Mary Sisler, Xavier Fourcade, Inc., New York

5 hearts» confront «the baby headlight» on the Jura-Paris road. The machine was Picabia's car, «a 5-cylinder which lashed out at a cogwheel.» Having conceived of the bride as a motor, in the shape of a tree, Duchamp racked his brain to see what form would be appropriate to her partner, the bachelor. He first made him «the head of 5 nudes,» that is to say the driver of a five-horsepower, on a road tending toward «a pure geometric line without thickness»; later he made him a motorcyclist (perkaps an analogy to the *Supermale* of Alfred Jarry), as attested to by his drawing, *To Have the Apprentice in the Sun* (see p. 49); here the bachelor is as virginal as the bride, an «apprentice» struggling to ascend a hill.

In the course of the year 1913, Duchamp became convinced that his personal inquiry into the nature of painting was over. Not only did he know of what the act of painting consisted, both in its traditional and innovative forms, but by this time he had acquired all the skills necessary to become a famous painter. A full member of the Autumn Salon, he could exhibit there each year without seeking anyone's approval. He was in a position to sell his paintings: Isadora Duncan had bought from him the small canvas of a nude. He was already being mentioned in art books: Gleizes and Metzinger, in *Concerning Cubism* (1912) had reproduced *Sonata* and the *Coffee Mill*. Finally, his boldest and most controversial executions had made him the center of public attention; in February, in New York, the Armory Show, the first large exhibition of modern painting in the United States, opened, and the spotlight was focused primarily on his *Nude Descending a Staircase*. Thousands of New Yorkers rushed to look at this scandalous picture about which everyone was talking. When the Armory Show moved to Chicago and to Boston, this success was repeated; as a result all four of the paintings which he was showing were soon bought by collectors. Duchamp was fully conscious of all this, and yet, at the precise moment when he might have begun an artistically prosperous career, this extraordinary man decided he would not take advantage of his fame in order to preserve his individuality.

No, he would not submit to a dull routine; he would not paint a monotonous succession of pictures in the same style to satisfy a clientele or win the support of reviewers. He would not apply himself to painting as if it were a manual trade from which to derive money and fame. Being interested only in intellectual adventure, in what a man could accomplish in the world by the use of his mind, he would throw himself into work which could not be classified or sold, which was unending and which resembled nothing conceived or painted before him, and in the course of this unique performance unfold all sorts of corollary ideas concerning the creative act. Since this decision definitely placed him beyond the pale of the commercial art market, he was obliged to seek employment; through the good offices of Maurice Davanne, Picabia's uncle, he was hired as librarian in the Sainte-Geneviève Library. This position enabled him to continue his cultural studies by reading the pre-Socratic Greek philosophers and various books on optics (among others the *Thaumaturgus Opticus* by Niceron).

In October 1913, escaping from the influence of his brothers, he rented a studio in Paris, 23 rue Saint-Hippolyte, and drew on the wall a complete outline of *The Bride Stripped Bare*. He sought to eliminate from the picture all sentimentality, all purely visual sensation, all taste. He wanted to prove that all the legitimate demands of art could be met by utilizing whatever was at hand, using the simplest of tools. Thus he attached a bicycle wheel to a kitchen stool; this object has not the significance of those which he subsequently used. It was the period when Delaunay and Kupka painted Newton's disks in order to express circular rhythms. Why paint disks, when one could put a bicycle wheel in one's studio and turn it when and as often as one wished? In the train taking him to Rouen, in January 1914, he passed the time retouching a vignette of a landscape; he added a red dot, a green dot, and called it *Pharmacy,* because these dots reminded him of the

MUSIQUE DE CHAMBRE

Chamber Music

LE MAESTRO DANS SES ŒUVRES
— ..... pour mourir dans un pianissimo.

Dessin de DUCHAMP

The Maestro and His Works
French Courier

EXPÉRIENCE

Experience

— Ce que t'es long à te peigner.
— La critique est aisée, mais la raie difficile.
Dessin de DUCHAMP.

«You're taking a long time to comb your hair.»
«Criticism's easy, but it's hard to make a part.»

— La morue est elle bien dessalée?...   Dessin de DUCHAMP.

«Is the cod unsalted? That is: Does it know a thing or two?»

Six cartoons which appeared in Laugh *and the* French Courier, *1907–1910*
National Library, Paris

Puree
French Courier

green and red globes to be seen at the time in pharmacists' windows. In his opinion, that was how one could make, without tiring oneself, something as worthwhile as any painting on display in an exhibition. What was painting? A certain way of retouching nature. And novelty in painting? Retouching the interpretation of nature made by various predecessors. One could be innovative only by building on the preceding works of others, themselves seen in relation to the works which preceded them.

The Bride Stripped Bare thus joined experiments that aimed to proclaim the uselessness of art. Duchamp bought a bottle rack and wrote on it an original phrase which served as a title. What good was it to work on a sculpture; here was one ready-made! A painted or sculptured work could be replaced by almost anything. Whereas an *invention,* such as the one he worked on while preparing his notes, with the seriousness of an engineer, could be found only in the head of a man.

At this point it is appropriate to anticipate and become acquainted with the general concept of the masterwork that would occupy him for eight years and become the principal myth of his life. He first thought about making it a painting on canvas; then, in order to avoid having to ink and fill out the canvas, he decided to paint on glass. To accustom himself to thinking of it as something other than a painting, he called it «a delay in glass,» indicating that he chose to «achieve with it a delay, as long as possible, in its general conclusion.» That meant that the careful development of the project would be slow and not subject to any constraints of time, and also that it was a delayed-action bomb, not causing an immediate outburst of hilarity such as a gag might produce, but provoking mirth by a ripening of the «irony of affirmation.»

This «delay in glass,» which was finally entitled *The Bride Stripped Bare by Her Bachelors, Even* (see p. 68), would be a demonstration of the following proposition: «Given 1) a waterfall and 2) illuminating gas, we can determine the conditions of the instantaneous Repose (or an allegorical appearance) of a succession (a collection) of divers facts, which appear by law and logic to depend on one another, and *isolate the signs of the consonance between,* on the one hand, this *Repose* (capable of innumerable eccentricities) and, on the other hand, a *Choice of Possibilities* legitimatized by these laws and also responsible for them.» The waterfall is the symbol of the female principle, the illuminating gas that of the male principle; the instantaneous (or extra rapid) Repose is the amorous ecstasy which results from their union; the studies of the possibilities of their meeting has as its goal to make clear «the signs of the consonance,» or that which makes the male principle indispensable to the female principle and vice versa. This painting on glass thus offers at once an image of the unconscious motivations which deepen the mystery of sexuality and the rudiments of a fantastic science which turns the very machines which it employs into objects of derision.

This prodigious enterprise ran into technical difficulties. How treat love in a comical manner without resorting to the «blue» jokes of burlesque? How integrate thought and language into painting without creating an anecdotal picture or one with a thesis? The sight of a chocolate grinder in action, in the window of a chocolate store in Rouen, furnished him with the solution. In 1913, a first painting in oil shows this object, mounted on a chassis with legs, style Louis XV; but its richness of form, its carefully drawn shadows, manage to give it decorative value. In February 1914, after two studies in pencil and oil (see p. 67) of the motor carriage of the machine, he executed *The Chocolate Grinder,* an example of «dry art,» completely impersonal; the streaks on the rollers are made with thread pasted and sewed on the canvas; the title is inscribed in gold letters on a black label. He would use *The Chocolate Grinder* as the central organ of the bachelor and as inspiration for the drawing of the whole. He would achieve the requisite dryness by placing graphics, equations and axioms confirming his hypotheses on working drawings or scraps of paper, as a scientist might.

PORTRAIT OF DR. R. DUMOUCHEL, 1910 Oil on canvas, 39³/₈″ × 25⁹/₁₀″
Philadelphia Museum of Art, The Louise and Walter Arensberg Collection

APROPOS OF LITTLE SISTER, 1911   *Oil on canvas,* 28¾″ × 23⅝″
Solomon R. Guggenheim Museum, New York

SONATA, 1911   Oil on canvas, $57\,^1/_{16}'' \times 44\,^1/_2''$
Philadelphia Museum of Art, The Louise and Walter Arensberg Collection

YOUNG MAN AND GIRL IN SPRING, 1911   Oil on canvas, 25⅞″ × 19¾″
Collection: Vera and Arturo Schwarz, Milan

To avoid any aestheticism, he would rely on chance. He would invent a new unit of length by dropping horizontally, from a height of one meter, three threads a meter in length. These three winding threads, each pasted on a strip of blue canvas and placed together in a croquet box, would form *The 3 Standard Stoppages* (see p. 59) «of chance in reserve.» The lines would be carried over to the *Network of Stoppages* (see p. 66) to describe the «capillary tubes» that feed the «malic» molds. Thus Duchamp, observing a rule of the game, is freed from the effort of correcting a stroke. In addition, to avoid any literary quality, he breaks up language and envisages the creation of an ideogrammatic alphabet, made of signs corresponding to all of the abstract words in the Larousse dictionary.

The confrontation of the Bride and her partner takes place on a large Glass, in algebraic manner. The Bride is on top, dominating the situation, for she is «an apotheosis of virginity.» She feels «ignorant desire, chaste desire (with a touch of mischievousness).» She is also called the Hanged Woman, since she is attached to a gallows of brilliant metal, which symbolizes «the attachment of the maiden to her parents and her friends.» This virginal machine consists of a motor of very feeble cylinder power, a superficial instrument activated by the fuel of love and exposed electric sparks; a magneto of desire which helps to lay base the electricity by throwing out sparks of continuing life; of a sort of tree which serves as a spinal column. The Bride also possesses «a milky way the color of flesh,» on which the bachelors can practice their «shooting» and cause a «moving inscription» to appear, with the aid of «pistons moved by air currents.»

Below, the bachelor-machine, «fat and lustful,» with an underpinning of masonry, has a motor of desire which, instead of being in direct contact with the Bride, is separated from her by a cooler with blades (or run by water). It includes a «Matrix of Eros,» consisting of eight «malic» molds corresponding to eight different liveries and uniforms (policeman, cavalryman, flunky, funeral director, constable, priest, delivery man, footman); these pieces are hollow and contain only illuminating gas, to which they will give eight «malic» forms. (Later he would envisage nine so as to have a multiple of three, the basic number of the Bride). As a matter of fact, the Bride is susceptible to the prestige of a uniform, which seems to her the mold of a true male; the *Cemetery of Uniforms and Liveries* (see p. 65) is the vague and tenuous image which she has of men, of which her suitor must remind her in order to win her.

The Matrix of Eros is fastened to a wagon with «shafts of freed metal,» concealing a water mill and animated by a descending weight; this wagon, whose runners slide in a gutter, goes back and forth in a «jolting rhythm,» while chanting the litany of a bachelor's life. But the soul of the bachelor-machine is the Chocolate Grinder, made up of rollers, a necktie and a bayonet which support the compression bar, scissors and insulating plates. The wagon, the Matrix of Eros and the Chocolate Grinder together produce a splash of liquid gas which shoots back toward a spot where it flows out, and is then directed toward the Bride by a reflection in the mirror of the «oculist's pictures.» A spring called a «handler of gravity,» a «combat marble» which, by bumping three times, releases the system of clockwork which removes the Bride's clothing, «sieves» in the form of semispherical parasols, a «wasp,» or sex cylinder, responsible for «feeding the fibrous matter,» complete this mechanism, whose operation will ensure the «crowning joy,» consisting of the joyous unfolding of the Bride who wants to be stripped bare, and of a similar ecstasy in the bachelor achieving his desire.

It would be inaccurate to think that Duchamp was describing two machines which he really wanted to construct and which would function publicly. Rather he was concerned by a mental construction which language, both pictorial and verbal, would set to working in the mind of the spectator. Duchamp built an experimental fable, in the same way that a philosopher or a scholar migth seek to understand mankind. He is the emulator of La Mettrie, who wrote *The Man-Machine* (1748) to prove that «organic matter in and of itself is endowed with motor power,» and especially of Condillac who, in his *Treatise on Sensation* (1754) imagined a statue which he limited in successive stages to the sense of smell, of hearing, of taste, of sight and of touch in order to explain what can be experienced with a single sense. He strikes it on the head and the feet, moves its arm, lifts it into the air, has it exposed to perfumes, noises, sources of heat and cold, and concludes what its reactions are. In the case of Condillac's statue, the dominant sense was touch, which taught the other senses how to judge external objects and develop curiosity; the Bride has the same tendency. One can also relate Duchamp's preoccupations to the experiments which the poet Charles Cros advocated in his *Principles of Cerebral Mechanics* (1879). Cros made use of kinetic inventions to demonstrate how the organs of perception function in man; thus he studied the physiology of sight thanks to a «device which was circular or had a turning pointer,» reproducing the manner in which colored images are transmitted from the retina to the brain. Duchamp, for his part, criticized the complexity of sexual activity in marriage through an apparatus which was the objective equivalent.

In a work in which text, drawing and painting on glass are inseparable, and allow us to contemplate *the inner working of a mind in movement,* the rupture with any precedents set in the history of painting is total. Nothing similar had ever been seen: a picture which, instead of decorating a wall, rises, transparent, in space, and whose elements, neither abstract nor realist, appear to be suspended in midair. Impossible to render an aesthetic judgment on this object; it is not subject to criteria of good and bad taste, to any concept of the beautiful, of technical skill, of sensitiveness of form. The Large Glass is a visible reminder of extraordinary research. Before executing his creations, Duchamp reviewed all the possible means of creating a work typical of the twentieth century, which owed nothing to the shibboleths of the past. Having chosen glass as his material, he proceeded to treat it in an entirely original way. At first he thought it enough to cover it with a coat of wax and to etch a design on it with fluor-hydrogenous acid; abandoning this procedure because of the noxious emanations, he pasted on lead wire, drawn out so that it could exactly define outlines. He silvered over that part depicting «oculist witnesses,» obtained the tint of the «sieves» by letting the dust which had been put on that spot several months earlier settle, and achieved the nine «shoots» by throwing nine matches against the glass and boring holes at the points of impact, etc. He pondered the most grandiose schemes: making «a hinged painting» which would open up like a folding ruler; using «colored flowers» and «*perfumes* (?) of red, blue, green and gray blending into yellow,» to which a phosphorescent substance would give the sheen of a luminous advertising sign. All of these speculations, revealed in his notes, involved the future of his art. It can thus be perceived that his subject implies, through his choice of the protagonists on a wedding night, the ambiguous relations of the Creator, his creation and the witnesses of the ravishing of the woman by the man. The Bride stripped bare by her bachelors is Painting stripped bare by those who paint and those who look at paintings.

*   *   *

When war was declared in 1914, Marcel Duchamp was not drafted as were his two brothers; exempt for reasons of health, he accepted the invitation of Walter Pach, who was organizing the Armory Show, to come to the United States. He landed in New York on June 15, 1915, and was immediately introduced to a couple of art collectors, Louise and Walter Arensberg, who lodged

La Joconde

L.H.O.O.Q., 1919 « Readymade » reproduction retouched in pencil, 7¾″ × 4⅞″
Private collection, Paris

For a Game of Chess, 1911   Charcoal and China ink on paper, 17^{11}/$_{16}$" × 24^{3}/$_{16}$"
Collection: Madame Marcel Duchamp, Villiers-sous-Grez

44

THE CHESS PLAYERS, 1911   Oil on canvas, $19^{11}/_{16} \times 24''$
National Museum of Modern Art, Paris

Yvonne and Magdeleine (Torn) in Tatters, 1911   Oil on canvas, 23⅝″ × 28¾″
Philadelphia Museum of Art, The Louise and Walter Arensberg Collection

Portrait (Dulcinea), 1911   Oil on canvas, 57½″ × 44⅞
Philadelphia Museum of Art, The Louise and Walter Arensberg Collectioi

46

To Have the Apprentice in the Sun, 1914
China ink and pencil on music paper,
10¾″ × 6¾″
Philadelphia Museum of Art,
The Louise and Walter Arensberg
Collection
▷

COFFEE MILL, 1911
Oil on canvas, 13″ × 4¹⁵/₁₆
Private collection

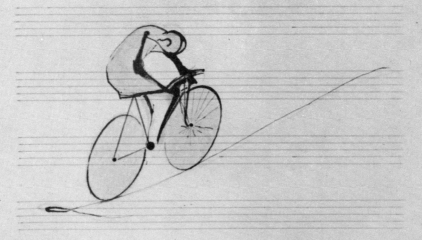

—avoir l'apprenti dans le soleil.—

Marcel Duchamp 1914.

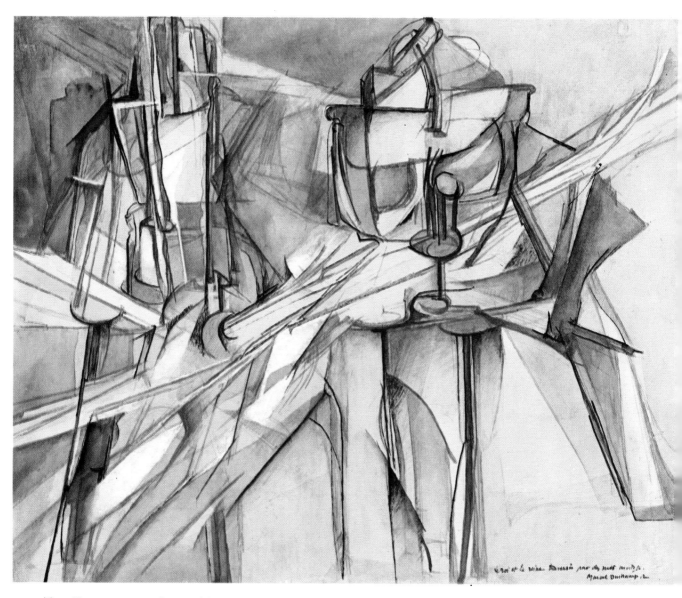

THE KING AND THE QUEEN TRAVERSED BY NUDES AT HIGH SPEED, 1912
Watercolor, pencil and gouache on paper, 19¼″ × 23¼″
Philadelphia Museum of Art, The Louise and Walter Arensberg Collection

▷

VIRGIN No. 2, 1912
Watercolor and pencil on paper, 15¾″ × 10⅛″
Philadelphia Museum of Art, The Louise and Walter Arensberg Collection

First sketch for The Bride Stripped Bare by Her Bachelors, 1912 Pencil and wash on paper, 9⅜" × 12⅝"
Collection: Cordier & Ekstrom, Inc., New York

Passage from the Virgin to the Bride, 1912   Oil on canvas, 23⅜″ × 21¼″
Museum of Modern Art, New York

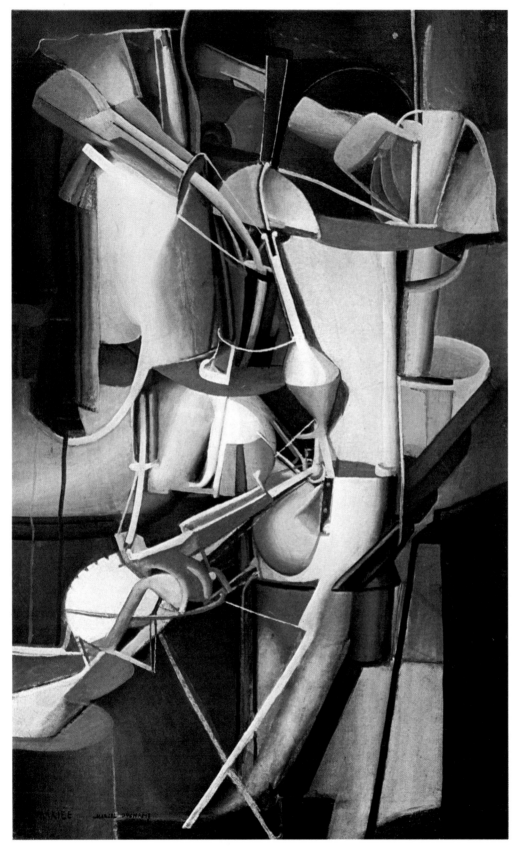

BRIDE, 1912
Oil on canvas,
35¼″ × 21⅝″
Philadelphia Museum
of Art, The Louise an
Walter Arensberg
Collection

NUDE DESCENDING A
STAIRCASE, No. 2, 1912
Oil on canvas,
57 1/2 × 35 1/16"
Philadelphia Museum of
Art, The Louise and
Walter Arensberg
Collection

SAD YOUNG MAN IN A TRAIN, 1911   Oil on canvas, 39⅜″ × 28¾″
Peggy Guggenheim Foundation, Venice

him in their apartment and became his enthusiastic patrons. As the creator of *Nude Descending a Staircase,* which was still a popular topic of conversation, he was welcomed as a conquering hero. He had no intention of profiting from this success and, true to his commitment not to live on the proceeds from his art, applied for a position as librarian at the French Institute. In September, the magazine *Art and Decoration* published the first interview with « Marcel Duchamp, iconoclast, » in which he expressed his joy at being in New York, which reminded him of the Paris of before the war. He became the idol of the group of poets and artists who assembled at the Arensbergs', among them, most notably, Joseph Stella, William Carlos Williams, Edgar Varèse, Arthur Cravan and his wife Mina Loy, Jean Crotti and Charles Demuth. It was there that he met Man Ray, who, like Picabia, would remain one of his dearest friends for the rest of his life.

Duchamp, as the most famous rebel in the modern art movement, was expected to take some revolutionary initiatives, and he did not disappoint these expectations. He set out to select manufactured objects which he could contrast with artistic creations and baptized them « readymades. » Very different from *The Bicycle Wheel* (see p. 83), which parodied Newton's disks, the readymades are « three-dimensional puns. » The first, born on American soil, is a snow shovel on which he wrote: « Before the broken arm. » Then came a metallic dog's comb entitled: « 3 or 4 driblets of height have nothing to do with savagery, » and the promotional picture for Sapolin paint transformed into *Apolinère Enameled* (see p. 77). Duchamp had a studio in the Lincoln Arcade Building, and set up on a trestle there two large glass panels so he could begin to paint *The Bride Stripped Bare.* He had affixed to the ceiling the pictures in his possession, as well as a hat rack; the bathtub was in the middle of the studio, and when he was taking a bath, he could open the door by pulling on a cord; a clothes tree attached to the floor was a stumbling block for visitors. On one occasion he spread out there his *Travel Sculpture,* made of strips of rubber. One could imagine oneself in the home of the skeptic Pyrrhon, who stated axiomatically: « Nothing is more this than it is that. » As a participant in a group show at the Bourgeois Gallery, Duchamp hung three readymades in the checkroom at the entrance; no one took any notice of them and looked all around for his works.

In 1916 he became one of the founders of the Society of Independent Artists, which had neither jury nor awards and, whose exhibitors were placed in alphabetical order; however, he hoped to achieve a sensational coup. He sent to the Salon of 1917 a urinal entitled *Fountain* and signed it R. Mutt. This provocatory act proved that he had gone on to still another period in his interrogation. After having asked himself what painting was, he posed to artists, if not to the general public, the question: *What is a work of art?* Could one create a work which was not art or practice art without creating a work? The response would be determined by the reactions of the spectators. But the members of the arrangements committee, embarrassed by this urinal which they could not refuse, in view of their own rules (they suspected the true identity of the exhibitor), hid it. As a protest, Duchamp resigned from the Society of Independent Artists, and in issue number 2 of his magazine *The Blind Man* (May 1917), commenting on a photograph, *Fountain,* by Alfred Stieglitz, he analyzed *The Case of Richard Mutt.* There could be only two reasons to reject the work, he claimed: either it was immoral and vulgar; or it plagiarized a plumbing accessory. Now, a urinal was no more immoral than a bathtub; it was an object to be seen in bathrooms every day. And the fact that Mr. Mutt had not made this « fountain » with his own hands was irrelevant; he had selected it. He had taken an everyday, commonplace object and treated it in such a way that its normal meaning had given way to another one, which was exclusively intellectual. Duchamp concluded: « The only works of art which America has contributed to society are its plumbing equipment and its bridges. » The urinal was an impertinent method of letting

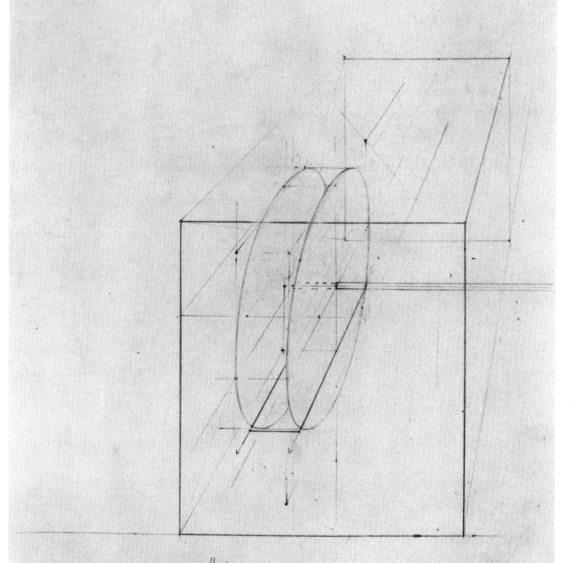

Projection d'ellipse = 12^{cm}

Rose trop petite (pour fournir force suffisante)   1913

à mon cher Hartl
affectueusement
1936.

Marcel Duchamp

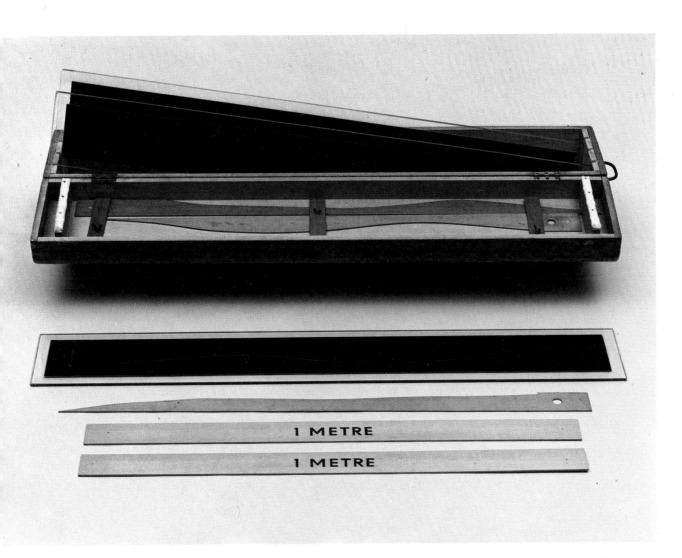

STANDARD STOPPAGES, 1913–14. Assemblage
Museum of Modern Art, New York, Katherine S. Dreier Bequest

Perspective Drawing for the Water Mill Wheel, 1913
Pencil on paper, 12" × 7¾"   Collection: Cordier & Ekstrom, Inc., New York

artists understand that a scorned utilitarian object was of more value than a canvas daubed without wit or originality. In an article in the same issue, *The Buddha of the Bathroom,* Louise Norton pointed out the absurdity of the reactions to Richard Mutt. «There are those who ask anxiously: 'Is he serious or is he joking?' Perhaps he is both at once! Is that not possible?» She refutes the argument that a thing cannot be an art object because it comes from a plumbing fixtures store. «I answer simply that *Fountain* was not done by a plumber, but was achieved through the force of a man's imagination.»

During this period Duchamp was earning a living by giving French lessons at two dollars an hour; among his pupils were the Stettheimer sisters: Carrie, Ettie and Florine. The charming bachelor was attractive to everyone, but especially to females; if he had wanted to marry, he could have made any number of good matches. Katherine S. Dreier, a wealthy heiress and abstract painter, was a fervent admirer. But he preferred to lead an existence of cocktail parties and costume balls, with all of the excesses they brought in their train. Henri-Pierre Roché, who observed him at this time, reported: «He began to drink a little too much. One night, at an artists' ball in Webster Hall, he stubbornly insisted on climbing to the top of the large flagpole in the middle of the room, a greasy pole bent at a 45-degree angle. Laboriously he made his way up, threatening to fall on the heads of the dancers. At last he succeeded, and everyone sighed with relief. Then, with a girl, he performed an unsteady balancing act beside the tracks of the elevated.» The way he gave up drink was typical. On one occasion, he and Roché left a reception completely drunk. «We zigzagged ahead. He observed: 'These zigzags are dangerous. They should be avoided.' After which he meticulously avoided them.» This man who refused to become a drunkard because of his desire to remain upright was also capable of cutting a straight path to attain an uncommon goal.

Meanwhile Duchamp continued to work on the Large Glass two hours a day, and for Katherine S. Dreier finished his last painting in oil, «*Tu m'*» (see pp. 78–79), an inventory of his concerns of the moment, in which he indicated that painting was the illusion of an illusion. Everything in «*Tu m'*» was reflection and pretense; in it he transposed readymades (the bicycle wheel, the hat rack), whose shadows he traced as they were thrown on the wall of his studio by a lamp. In the lower left, he placed a picture of the *3 Standard Stoppages.* In the center of the picture, a tear was camouflaged by the use of the *trompe-l'œil* technique, and then he added two real safety pins to make it seem like an actual tear. A series of colored squares, reproduced in a catalogue, were fastened with a pin. A hand, which he had drawn by a sign painter, pointed with a finger toward a maze of lines. By this Duchamp was stating that a picture should not be observed to see if it was beautiful or ugly, if what it represented was false or true; he was trying to force the spectator to decide for himself why he was looking at the painting. If he was mystified, so much the better; if he was scandalized his awareness would be stimulated, and he would be forced to take a position. As for Duchamp, sight was a dual sense. «One can look at someone seeing; one cannot listen to someone listening.» That is why he put a magnifying glass in the center of his study on glass: *To Be Looked at (from the Other Side of the Glass) with One Eye, Close to, for Almost an Hour,* which he did in Buenos Aires, where he stayed for nine months beginning in August 1918. Nothing appears under the magnifying glass, which proves simply that a work is executed to look at the spectator looking, or to see the artist look.

Meanwhile Dada had burst forth in Switzerland, where Tristan Tzara, in his *1918 Manifesto,* called for an all-out revolt against all artistic schools. During a brief trip to France, in October 1919, Duchamp touched up a reproduction of the *Mona Lisa,* to which he added a moustache and a goatee. This picture, which he entitled *L.H.O.O.Q.* (see p. 43) would become the Dada emblem.

If one thinks about it, one realizes that this action is not comparable to that of a child who playfully disfigures the portraits in his textbooks. It implies a disrespectful judgment on art and history and sheds unexpected light on Leonardo da Vinci. When Picabia wanted to reproduce this retouched Mona Lisa in *391*, he did not have it on hand and therefore did another, forgetting the goatee; this imperfect version, if compared with the original, shows how much stronger Duchamp's version was. It reveals even more effectively than a Freudian analysis Leonardo da Vinci's homosexuality; it shows that he painted the Mona Lisa because she reminded him of a man, as Proust described Albert under the mask of Albertine. With a few strokes of the pen Duchamp said more than a thick volume could have; his action was an act of expert criticism. At the same time he was denouncing the hypocrisy of works of art, pointing out that the image before which the crowd kneels adoringly is not at all the one with which the artist was secretly preoccupied.

Duchamp returned to New York in January 1920, taking to Walter Arensberg a vial containing *50 cubic centimeters of Paris air,* and keeping in touch with Picabia, who had become associated with the group of *Literature* founded by André Breton and had thrown himself into a succession of Dadaist demonstrations. In the United States, Duchamp had no difficulty representing Dada, of which he had been the predecessor. In his studio, with the assistance of Man Ray, he constructed his first optical machine, *Revolving Sheets of Glass* (see p. 73), consisting of five plates covered with black and white lines which, while turning on an axis, formed continuous circles. How inconsistent is art, which tends to satisfy the sensation of sight, since it is possible to invent machines which continue to stimulate this sensation indefinitely! Duchamp then directed his activity to « the quest of the anti-masterpiece, » as Gabrielle Buffet would say. Thus, it was not enough for him to have made fun of the Joconda and cast some doubt on the creator's true intent; he wanted to create an anti-Joconda. She would be an imaginary woman who would fascinate the present generation even more than da Vinci's model had. He would call her Rose Sélavy, derived from the axiom: Life is no good (« *Rosse est la vie* »); then Rrose Sélavy, because she advised men: « Drink — that's life » (« *Arrose, c'est la vie* »). Unnecessary to paint her portrait, in a century when photography shared the laurels with painting; Rose Sélavy, the anti-Joconda, would be Marcel Duchamp himself, masquerading as a woman and photographed by Man Ray. And to prove that indeed she was alive, he would credit her with some readymades and some witticisms; the first readymade to read, « copyright Rose Sélavy, » would be *Fresh Window,* a window with leather panes. A new portrait of her would decorate the perfume bottle, « Fresh Breath, Veiling Water, » reproduced in April 1921 in the one issue to appear of *New York Dada* (see p. 74).

In June 1921, Duchamp returned to Paris for a stay of six months at the home of his sister Suzanne, who was remarried to Jean Crotti. He attended the gatherings of the *Literature* group and strongly impressed André Breton, who saw in him a dandy whose « admirable beauty » he saluted; also « elegance of the most fatal sort. » In the article which Breton devoted to him shortly afterward, he added that this power lay in « his *disdain of dogma,* an attitude astonishing to those less favored. » Duchamp's role as a dandy was a way of announcing to the public that the only true art was the art of living. Whether he astounded by his paintings or by his conduct, it amounted to exactly the same thing. Breton bore witness to this. « I have seen Duchamp do something extraordinary: throw a coin in the air, saying: 'Heads I leave this evening for America; tails I stay in Paris.' This did *not* display indifference; undoubtedly he vastly preferred to leave, or to stay. » When Georges de Zayas drew a comet on his head with a razor and decorated his tonsure with a star, Duchamp was illustrating the culmination of « dry art »: to make a living work of oneself. Similarly, when he manufactured a giant check to pay his dentist, he was, according to his own statement, an « influential adventurer, in his hours of affluence. »

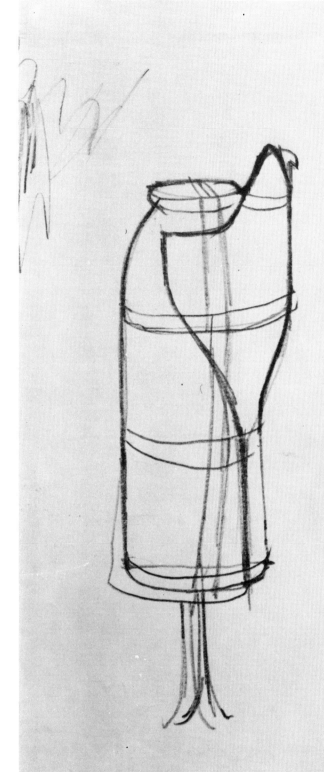

Chef 1 gare

marcel Duchamp
1913

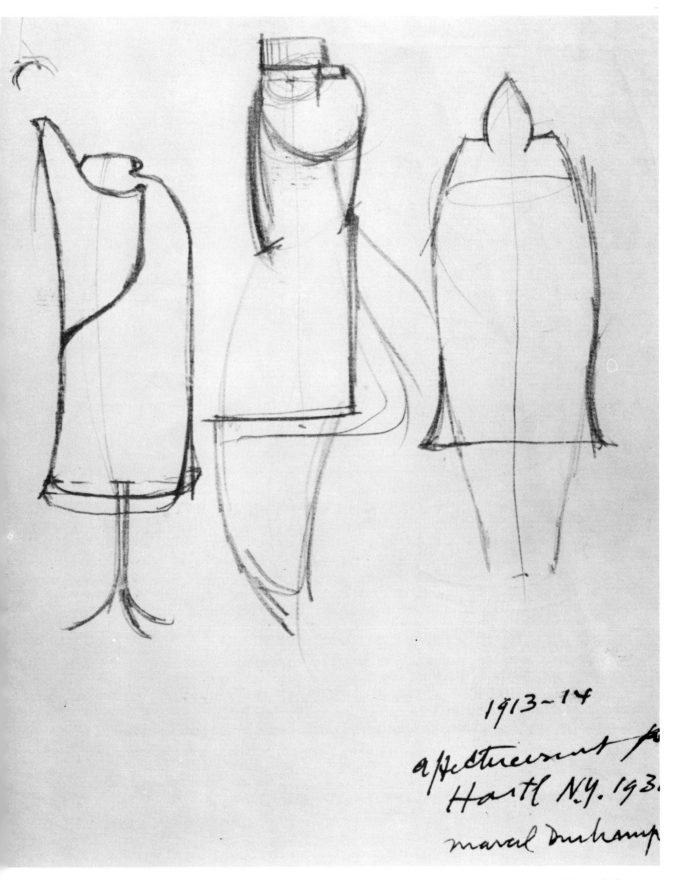

1913-14

affectueuse... f...

Harth N.Y. 193.

marcel duchamp

Studies for the «Bachelors,» 1913   Pencil drawings on two sides of paper,   8³/₈" × 6¹/₂"
Collection: Cordier & Ekstrom, Inc., New York

In January 1922, once again in New York, Duchamp concentrated on finishing the Large Glass, while working all year on the Oculist Witnesses, a construction which aimed to reflect the «sculpture of drops» which had splattered. He had silver foil applied to it in a factory in Long Island; then he exposed the design by a long and painstaking scratching procedure. At the beginning of 1923, Duchamp suddenly ceased his work on the Large Glass, which he signed and entrusted to Katherine S. Dreier, who had bought it from him. It was supposed that he had left *The Bride Stripped Bare* unfinished, and he himself did nothing to discredit this rumor. In fact, the work could not be finished, since he had undertaken it in order to prove that in painting the concept is more valuable than the realization. His Large Glass is an inventory of his intentions rather than a vindication of material values. If in it he did not include certain elements which had been anticipated — the Toboggan, the Prize Fight, the Juggler of Centers of Gravity, the picture of cast Shadows — they are present in filigree in the general composition.

Duchamp was eager to make a painting without canvas, without brushes, without an external model and with uncertain colors, integrating into it dust, rust, red lead and silver foil. Now even this painting of the impossible no longer seemed very attractive to him. He decided to return to Europe and to shed his old skin there, so that in the future they could say of him: The painter is dead; long live the man!

*   *   *

In Paris, Duchamp found that the cycle of Dada had almost come to an end, but that nothing yet had been introduced to succeed it. Taking up residence at the Istria Hotel, rue Campagne-Première, he entered a period during which he answered the question: *How can one express oneself better than through literature and the plastic arts?*

In 1924 he worked on a new optical machine, for which he had procured an order from the couturier, Jacques Doucet. This consisted of a demiglobe with spirals that turned on a foundation of brass and was activated by an electric motor and balanced on a leg kept secure by a wooden triangle. On October 21 he informed Doucet: «Today I brought the exterior brass plate to the engraver, who is to engrave a sentence in circular form. This, and a work with a mottled effect which I myself will draw on the brass, will give the object, even when it is not moving, a curious appearance. For, as you very astutely remarked, it could be monotonous to watch it turn continuously.» Duchamp intended that this globe be an optical game for the public without any artistic pretensions. Asked to loan it to an exhibition (probably the first Surrealism show, at the Pierre Gallery), he confessed to Doucet his reluctance to show it: « All the exhibitions of painting and sculpture nauseate me. And I have no desire to participate in them.»

That same year he worked on inventing a system to win at roulette in Monte Carlo. After trying out his formula for five days at the casino and regularly winning small amounts, he wrote Picabia: «As you see, I have not stopped being a painter; now I draw on my luck.» In spite of some disappointing results, he formed a society for the promotion of roulette in Monte Carlo, for which the debenture was a colored lithograph so extraordinary that Jane Heap commented in *The Little Review*: «Anyone who wishes to invest some money in aesthetic curiosities will find in it the answer to a prayer. The signature of Marcel alone is worth considerably more than the 500 francs being asked.» Toward the end of 1925 Duchamp gave up the ambitious project to force roulette into the mold of a chess game. At least his experience in Monte Carlo was proof that he intended to substitute for the personage of the artist that of the gambler rising above good fortune

CEMETERY OF UNIFORMS AND LIVERIES, THE BACHELORS, 1914
Pencil, ink and watercolor on paper, 26″ × 39⅜″
Yale University Art Gallery, Gift of Katherine S. Dreier for the Corporation Collection, U.S.A.

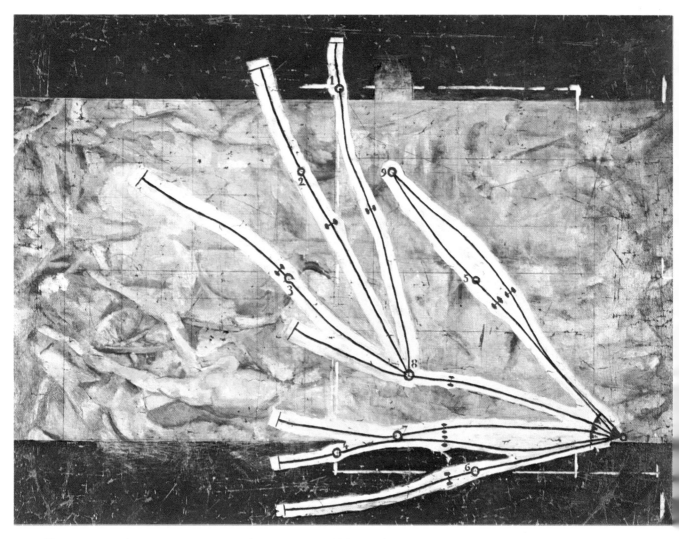

NETWORK OF STOPPAGES, 1914   Oil on canvas, 58$^1/_8$″ × 77$^9/_{16}$″
Museum of Modern Art, New York, Abby Aldrich Rockefeller Fund and Gift of Mary Sisler

THE CHOCOLATE GRINDER, 1914   Oil and pencil on canvas, 28$^3/_4$″ × 23$^5/_8$′
Kunstsammlung, Nordrhein-Westfalen, Düsseldorf

BRIDE STRIPPED
BARE BY HER
OWN BACHELORS, F
(THE LARGE GLASS
1915–1923
Oil and lead on gla.
109¼″ × 69¼″
Philadelphia Museu.
of Art,
Katherine S. Dreier
Bequest

and bad. The goal sought in his Large Glass had become his life's goal: *to become the master of chance.*

When Surrealism was born, Duchamp kept his distance and as a result could not claim to be considered a hero by its founders. Breton, in his *Manifesto,* described him as a visitor to the château which Breton and his friends occupied. «Last week, in the gallery of mirrors, we received someone named Marcel Duchamp who had not been known to us.» None of his works were reproduced in the twelve issues of *The Surrealist Revolution,* and he was mentioned only once, as «an intelligence unwilling to *serve,*» with the reproach that he was unwilling to explain why. It was because Duchamp was devoting himself exclusively to chess, no longer as an amateur but as a professional; instead of exhibiting readymades, he was exhibiting himself in tournaments. For him, the supreme creative act was no longer performed on paper or on glass, but on a chessboard whose pieces he manipulated. This attitude implied a lively criticism of contemporary artists, to whom he appeared to be saying: «As long as you do not produce art which is as real and as absorbing as a chess game, I will not agree to play with you.» He kept away from the Surrealists because of their political activity, which was at odds with his absolute refusal to become involved, and suggested that painters and poets should take as their model the chess player, concentrating impassibly, indifferent to what might be going on around him, using a combination of moves to achieve his end.

Nevertheless, between two matches, Duchamp quietly reminded the public that his renunciation of art was only conditional and temporary. He participated in the filming of *Anemic Cinema,* a seven-minute movie which featured his disks with spirals, enlivened by puns. He worked on the catalogue of a sale of Picabia's art with a preface signed Rrose Sélavy and attempted to popularize Brancusi in the United States. He helped Katherine S. Dreier organize some lectures and exhibitions for the Corporation, of which he was the permanent secretary; but it was without his consent that she loaned *The Bride Stripped Bare* to the Brooklyn Museum in November 1926 for an international exhibition of modern art. The Large Glass was broken while it was being shipped by truck, after the show, from the museum to Katherine S. Dreier's house in Connecticut. A few years later, in tears, she informed him of this, but he consoled her — a philosopher who believed that «men are mortal, also pictures»; earlier, when he saw that his little glass *«Malic» Molds* was cracked, he had said: «Finally!»

Duchamp's actions and gestures were closely studied by *avant-garde* connoisseurs, who saw in them the signs of a tranquilly subversive mind. In order to have more space, he used only one door of his studio on the rue Larrey; shortly after he moved in, *Orbs* reproduced in detail the arrangements of the rooms, explaining: «When one opens one door to enter the room, it blocks the entrance to the bathroom, and when one opens the door which leads to the bathroom, it closes the door of the studio, and is painted with white enamel paint like the inside of the bathroom.» Duchamp was hailed as an ever ingenious inventor, who this time had «found a way of constructing a door which is at the same time open and shut.»

In 1932 Duchamp had published, together with Vitaly Halberstadt, *The Opposition and the Joined Squares Are Reconciled,* which treated a situation common at the end of chess games, when there remain only pawns which are blocked and the two kings. Pierre de Massot, in the summer of 1933, revealed to the readers of *Orbs* that the printing of this book was admirably recherché. «To prove my thesis I need only point to the type of the title on the cover. Formed of stenciled letters in zinc, 8 to 10 centimeters high, such as are used on packing cases, the title was placed between two sheets of glass and, at a sloping angle, exposed to the sun. The *uncontrollable* distortion produced on the ground by the sun's rays hitting the hollows in the letters was photographed by Duchamp, who later made a negative from this photo which became a printing plate. I should also mention the admirable folding transparencies (diagrams) which explain visually some long and complicated theoretical principles.»

At the insistence of his friends, Duchamp agreed to publish his notes for *The Bride Stripped Bare by Her Own Bachelors;* the fact that he saw, in October 1933, the damage suffered by his Large Glass persuaded him also to make public the concept behind this panel, in case it might disappear completely. The result was *The Green Box,* in a printing of three hundred copies by Editions Rrose Sélavy; in it he assembled pell-mell facsimiles of his torn, stained memos, scrawled in pencil or in ink, covered with strokes of red and green and illustrated with graphics. The rectangular cardboard that served as the cover bore the title, pricked in holes made by a stylus-like instrument. The idea of publishing the scraps of his experimentation haphazardly, without order or organization, was resented as an outrageous and unforgivable performance, and Jacques-Henry Lévesque saw in it «the suppression of the intermediary step between manifestations of life and men.» One can date Duchamp's participation in Surrealism from the publication of *The Green Box* in September 1934. André Breton had published some excerpts in issue No. 5 of *Surrealism in the Service of the Revolution* a few months earlier; and subsequently, in *Minotaur,* his article, *Beacon of the Bride,* would make Duchamp a hero of the surrealist pantheon.

The first work created by Duchamp in the surrealist style was the series of his *Rotoreliefs* in 1935; they illustrated a fundamental feature of the surrealist spirit: «the appeal of the supernatural.» They were six cardboard disks, on which were drawn twelve designs in color with a spiral base; placed on a phonograph turntable with a speed of 35 revolutions a minute, they gave the impression of expanding forms. One might believe that they were simply a variation of the optical disks of 1923, reproduced in *Anemic Cinema.* But the former disks were abstract, whereas the *Rotoreliefs* changed into flowers, fish, a champagne glass, and gave the spectator the pleasure of seeing something inert and meaningless turn into something animate and fairylike. The twelve designs reproduced on the *Rotoreliefs* were entitled: *Corolla, Boiled Egg, Chinese Lantern, Lamp, Japanese Fish, Snail, Bohemian Glass, Hoops, Montgolfier Balloon, Cage, Eclipse, White Spiral.* Duchamp himself displayed his *Rotoreliefs* in a stand of the Concours Lépine at the Porte de Versailles; smiling and glib, he demonstrated his disks, making them turn either vertically or horizontally. He was located between a man who was selling a machine to compress garbage, thanks to a pressure screw which reduced it to small combustible cones, and a woman who was offering an instant potato peeler which functioned like a pencil sharpener. Alas! The public went directly from the machine to compress garbage to the potato peeler without ever stopping before Duchamp's stand; the appeal to the wondrous and the marvelous echoed on the empty air.

Henceforth Duchamp became a powerful force in the surrealist movement and counter-balanced the rigidity of Breton, compared with whom he represented a superb example of airy ease in assessing moral and aesthetic values. He took part in the surrealist exhibitions in Tenerife and in London, in the showing of surrealist objects at Ratton's in Paris. The chess game was in competition with the game of art without art; during the summer of 1936, he restored the Large Glass in the house of Katherine S. Dreier in West Redding, redoing the inscription at the top, the section of the nine shootings, the clothes of the Bride, and reinforcing the whole with a brace. In February 1937, his first one-man show opened without him at the Arts Club in Chicago; the same year he collaborated in the decoration of the bookstore-gallery Gradiva, managed by Breton, on the rue de Seine. It was he who designed the door, cutting the glass pane in such a way that it suggested the double silhouette of a couple embracing (see p. 80). A symbolic act: it occurred to Duchamp he could suggest *how to enter* into Surrealism, and in general into any adventure of the heart and mind. He was officially assigned this role when he was named «chief arbitrator» of the 1938 surrealist exhibition at the Beaux-Arts Gallery; those inventions of his which astounded

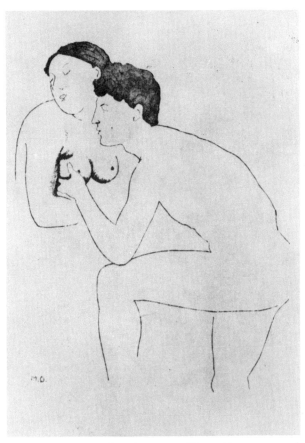

Pastiche of Ingres, II, 1968
Etching, $19^{7}/_{8}'' \times 12^{4}/_{5}''$

Pastiche of Courbet, 1968
Etching, $19^{7}/_{8}'' \times 12^{4}/_{5}''$

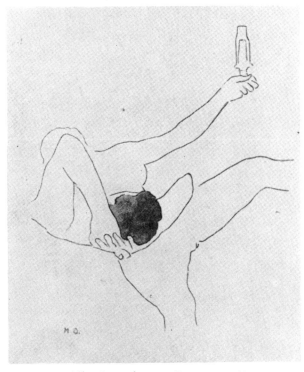

The Incandescent Burner, 1968
Etching, $19^{7}/_{8}'' \times 12^{4}/_{5}''$

The Bride Stripped Nude . . .
Etching, $19^{7}/_{8}'' \times 12^{4}/_{5}''$

Pastiches: reproductions of illustrations in book by Arturo Schwarz: «The Large Glass and Related Works, Vol. II»

*Discs Bearing Spirals, 1923   Ink and pencil on paper, each circle
having a diameter between 8¹/₂" × 12¹/₂" on a sheet of paper 42³/₅" × 42³/₅"
Seattle Art Museum, Eugene Fuller Memorial Collection, U.S.A.*

Revolving Sheets of Glass, Precision Optics, 1920   Optical motor engine, 47½″ × 72½″
Yale University Art Gallery, Gift of the Corporation Collection, U.S.A.

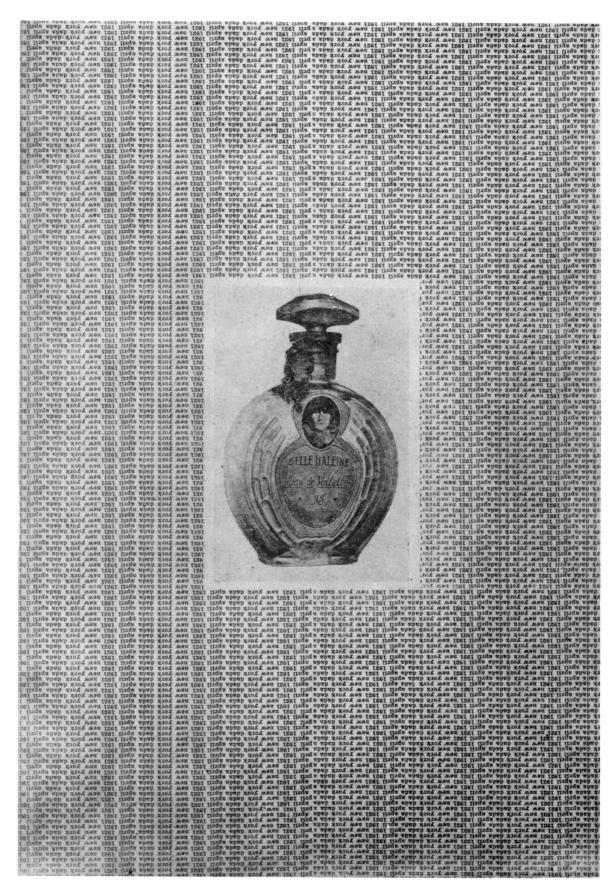

Cover for New York Dada, 1912   14½″ × 10″
Collection: Xavier Fourcade, Inc., New York

Monte Carlo Bond, 1924   Photo-collage on lithograph, $12^3/_8$" $\times$ $7^{11}/_{16}$"
Museum of Modern Art, New York, Gift of the artist

«Why Not Sneeze Rose Sélavy?» 1921 «Readymade», 4^1/$_2$" × 8^5/$_8$" × 6^5/$_{16}$"
Philadelphia Museum of Art, The Louise and Walter Arensberg Collection

APOLINÈRE ENAMELED, 1916–1917   « Readymade » Girl in a Bedstand, 9⅝″ × 13⅜″
Philadelphia Museum of Art, The Louise and Walter Arensberg Collection

« Tu m'. . . », 1918
Oil and pencil on canvas, with brush and two safety pins and another pin, 27½″ × 122¾″
Yale University Art Gallery, Katherine S. Dreier Bequest, U.S.A.

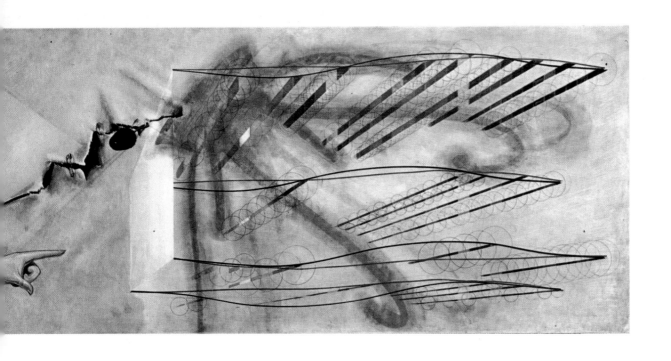

DOOR FOR GRADIVA, 1930–1968   Plexiglass, 78″ × 52″
Collection: Dieter and Miriam Keller, Stuttgart

Given 1) the waterfall, 2) the illuminating gas . . . , 1946–68   Assemblage, 95½″ × 70″ × 49″
Philadelphia Museum of Art, Gift of the Cassandra Foundation

the public, such as the 1200 bags of coal suspended on the ceiling of a grotto illuminated by a brazier, the revolver racks on which to affix drawings, the street of all the Devils, showed to what an extent he envisaged himself the stage director of the interior life.

Nevertheless, to prove conclusively that he no longer intended to create, Duchamp wished to see published an edition of his complete works. Such a man was evidently not going to be content with a simple illustrated volume, the pages of which one could turn by hand. He invented a «portable museum,» assembling in a valise of fawn leather sixty-nine phototype reproductions, four pages of text, four objects smaller than life-size and a replica of the Large Glass on celluloid. Each *Box-in-a-valise* contained one original and bore the name of the recipient. Of the three hundred projected, only twenty valises were made up in 1941. War was raging at that moment, and Duchamp, after crossing occupied France by pretending to be a cheese salesman, arrived in Marseilles with the intention of going back to the Unites States. His baggage was that of a merchant of lost illusions; like Ubu, who carried his conscience folded in a suitcase, this traveler had in his hand the bits and pieces of his Genius.

*   *   *

On June 25, 1942, Duchamp landed in New York, where this time he established a permanent residence. He became a member of the group of Surrealists in exile, participating in the founding of the magazine *VVV* and helping Breton organize the exhibition, *First Papers of Surrealism,* in October, in order to proclaim that in spite of the war, the life of the spirit, with its protest against sordidness and its hope in the wondrous side of life, continued. Duchamp had hung in the interior of the gallery a number of cords interlaced like the mesh of a net, which made it difficult to get near the works and thus suggested that the discovery of artistic creations demanded of the discoverer that he defy taboos and brush aside ambushes. The catalogue, one side of which suggested a wall riddled by bullets, the other a piece of Gruyère cheese, announced: «Opening dedicated to children playing under aromatic cedars.» Indeed, Duchamp wanted visitors to be disturbed, on the day of the official opening, by children playing the most boisterous games.

Selected by all the Surrealists to be their scout and their arbitrator, he led a monastic existence in a studio containing a table, a single chair, a packing case which served as an additional seat, a bed and bare walls on which a scrap of string hung on a nail. One could only communicate with him by letter or telegram, since he had no telephone. He read books which discussed various chess problems and played them out for about four hours each day. He made a pocket chess set, «which resists bumps and jolts,» on which the pawns were secured by pressure buttons. When he intervened in art matters, as he did infrequently, he invariably created a sensation. The magazine *Vogue* ordered from him a cover for its issue of July 4, 1943; he created *Genre Allegory* (see p. 88), a portrait of George Washington in the shape of a map of the United States, his face a banner with stars, against a background of sky-blue cardboard. But in the collage he used bandages whose red stains looked like blood; the magazine's editorial staff, afraid it would shock the public, refused to use the cover. Duchamp also did some window displays for Brentano's Bookstore; his display for *Arcanum 17* by Breton, which included a decapitated female mannequin with a faucet sticking out of her thigh, brought a protest from a feminist group. Finally, he collaborated with Hans Richter on the film, *Dreams That Money Can Buy* (1944), in which *Rotoreliefs* could be seen in action and there was also a showing of *Nude Descending a Staircase.* Duchamp, who in his youth had considered becoming a film technician, later worked with Richter

Bicycle Wheel, 1951   Assemblage, 25½″ and 23⅔″, 49⅛″ in height
Museum of Modern Art, New York, Gift of Sidney and Harriet Janis

on an unfinished film, *8 × 8,* in which the roles of chess pawns were interpreted by unpaid volunteer actors.

Denis de Rougemont, who spent a few days with Duchamp in a house on Lake George in August 1945, was fascinated by him, finding him an ascetic who possessed a transcendental wisdom and expressed amazing opinions on society, studying what he called the *infra-slight,* that is to say the extreme limit of the perceptible, of all the senses: for example, the noise made by his ribbed velvet trousers when he walked. He believed that all creative paths should lead to the expression of the infra-slight. When the surrealist group, reunited in Paris after the war, affirmed that it still endured by an exhibition in 1947 at the Maeght Gallery, Duchamp made visible there the infra-slight of humor with the room of Superstitions, the multicolored rain curtains that one had to skirt to reach, without disturbing the billiard players, the unprecedented labyrinth, the cover in the shape of a breast with the instruction: *Please touch.*

From that time on Duchamp's existence became more and more mythical, as he was present even when absent and inspired others to be inventive by virtue of his example. The year 1954 marked a late turning point in his life. At the age of sixty-seven he married, offering as a wedding present to his wife Alexina the object, *Corner of Chastity,* a sequel to his sculptures in galvanized plaster, *Female Vine Leaf and Dart-Object.* A naturalized American, Duchamp became fashionable because of the room devoted to his works in the Philadelphia Museum, which accepted the Arensberg collection. The public was exposed to his Large Glass, and the reviews of this strange creation began to proliferate. This painter who did not paint, influenced painting as much as a Picasso; the abstract Expressionists, along with Willem de Kooning, paid him homage, not because he had ever produced anything resembling their output, but because he made anything possible; Rauschenberg, Jasper Johns and the Pop artists, Arman, Tinguely and the exponents of the «New Realism» laid claim to his support; during his summertime visits to Cadaquès, Dali was lavish in his admiration. Duchamp continued to be severe in his judgments on ambitions which he considered too limited in scope, congratulating the Surrealists on their integrity in a letter to *Medium.* «It is a real pleasure for me to see that there exists in Paris something other than art merchandise. (Ed. note: *Arassuxait,* read phonetically, is *art à succès.*) Paraphrasing Jarry, one might contrast contemporary academism with 'PatArt.' Unfortunately, Picabia is no longer with us to act as a PatArtist.»

Toward the end of his life Duchamp gave numerous interviews to explain his past attitudes, but it would be a mistake to take them too seriously. He had reshuffled his cards, and the comments of his old age cast a feeble and misleading light on his frame of mind in his youth; nothing in them frees scholars from the need to consult their own intuitive findings. Their most positive aspect is their intellectual liveliness, which time had not impaired. This explains the originality of the debate which he stimulated during this period and which revolved around the question: *Who is the author of a picture?* Before him, that question had been posed only by experts whose function was to issue certificates of authenticity. But to Duchamp all pictures were fakes; the originals remained concealed in the recesses of the human mind. That led him to the conclusion: «It is the *observers* who make pictures. Today they are discovering El Greco; the public is painting his pictures three hundred years after their titular author.» In 1957, in a lecture in Houston on *The Creative Process,* he defined the «coefficient of art» as not only the difference between the artist's concept and its eventual realization, but also as the difference between the realization and its interpretation by the spectator.

Apparently Duchamp was simply a man who presided at banquets, at exhibitions, and made provocative statements, sometimes defining himself as an *anartist,* sometimes as a *respirator.* From time to time a readymade, a plastic sculpture, a drawing was a reminder that he still possessed

The Box of 1932, 11¾″ × 18¼″ × 3½″
Collection: Xavier Fourcade, Inc., New York

a masterful touch. He signed the two copies that Ulf Linde and Richard Hamilton respectively made of the Large Glass; he authorized Arturo Schwarz to reproduce some of his old readymades in limited quantities. In 1914, had he himself not invented « multiples » with the three copies of *Pharmacy*? On the invitation to his exhibition at Cordier and Ekstrom in 1965, he had the Joconda reproduced just as it was, with the notation: « Shaven » (Ed. note: The word « rasée » can also mean « bored stiff »). This amoral individual expressed his philosophy through objects as Chamfort did through aphorisms.

Although Marcel Duchamp was honored everywhere as a wise man who had contempt for the fruitless ferment of artistic movements, he was secretly preparing a surprise for his admirers: he was drawing up his will in the form of a last invention and giving its contemplators a lesson to ponder over. For twenty years, from 1946 to 1966, he worked on this project, assembling its constituent parts in a building on 14th Street in New York without letting anyone know except for his wife and the executor of the will, William N. Copley. It was neither a painting nor a sculpture, but rather an environmental construction or, according to his definition, a « dismountable likeness, » which could be taken apart and put together again anywhere at all. He gave it the title: *Given 1) the waterfall, 2) illuminating gas* (see p. 81), which was the start of the motif of the Large Glass, and thereby indicated his desire to make it the sequel and the logical conclusion of the allegory of the Bride.

Duchamp's visual will appears the most banal thing in the world. One is before a wall, in the center of which is a barn door, bordered by two brick columns and a brick arch and permanently closed by two cross-bars. As a matter of fact, there are no latches with which to open it, and the wooden planks, badly squared off, do not permit the onlooker to see through the cracks. To the naked eye it is a door which serves only to point the way to an unusable site; the sensible visitor will not try to enter and will continue on his way. However, if he is curious, he will notice that two of the nails can be pulled out; and that through the holes which they covered, which are at eye level, filters a faint light. If he looks through the tiny openings, he will be astounded; across the break in the wall he will see a disquieting scene. A nude woman lies upside down on a pile of twigs, her legs spread wide; her sexual area is hairless like that of a young girl, but her bosom is fully developed. Except for a few blonde tresses one cannot see her head or her right arm; in her left hand she holds an incandescent burner which is lit. In the background, a landscape of forests and hills, with a waterfall flowing into a pond, is irradiated by a fairylike light cast by the sky and the shimmering waters. An effect of anguish, of mystery and of voluptuousness which each person can interpret differently emanates from the scene. What has taken place? A rape? A crime? Some perverse kind of game? Is the woman a solitary bather drying herself in the sun, or is she sleeping in a garden? Is her gesture a distress signal or a call to arms? If Duchamp took a long time to create this image, it is precisely because he wanted it to be altogether ambiguous, so that one might see in it either the body of a raped girl or of a nymphomaniac. He was putting the spectator to a test, forcing him to reveal his or her own unconscious desires at the very moment when the spectator thought he was merely analyzing the intention of the artist.

Duchamp added instructions on how to use this « dismountable likeness, » indicating, in thirty-five pages of notes and a hundred and sixteen photos which he himself had taken, how to perform the fifteen operations needed to reassemble it. He went into the most infinitesimal detail, specifying that it should take two people to lift the nude woman and drawing attention to six « bushes » in the pile of branches on which she is stretched out. The magician cynically revealed all of his tricks, but not his intention. What was the message which Duchamp wanted to send us in *Given 1) the waterfall, 2) illuminating gas*? It cannot be found in the component objects in the work, since he purposely made it possible to attribute to these different and mutually inconsistent

The King Checked by the Queen, undated   Pencil on paper, 7⅛" × 6½"
Collection: Xavier Fourcade, Inc., New York

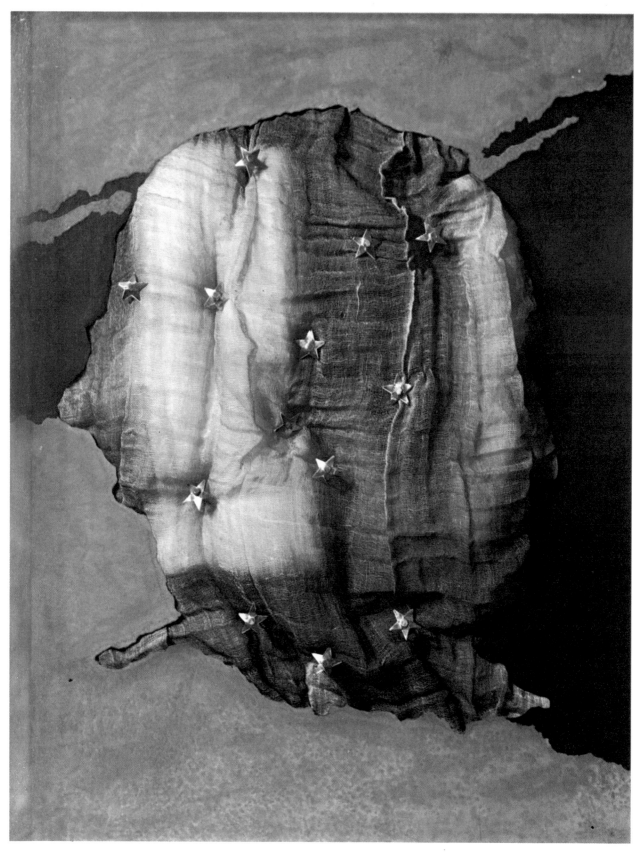

Genre Allegory (George Washington), 1943   Assemblage, $20^{15}/_{16}'' \times 15^{15}/_{16}''$
Private collection

meanings. It would be futile to try to determine if he was seeking to suggest a bride finally stripped bare or the victim of a sadist. The gesture of the woman brandishing an incandescent burner parodies, at ground level, that of the Statue of Liberty raising her torch at the entrance to New York Harbor. This similarity was certainly not involuntary and leads one to conclude that his aim was to pay homage to the liberty of the creative artist. The artist was free to make whatever he wished, and the spectator was free to see in it whatever suited his fancy. At the same time Duchamp symbolized the relation of the so-called art lover to a work of art; he passed in front of it, indifferent, not realizing that it could offer unsuspected pleasure. Whether he noticed by himself (innate curiosity) or was alerted by others (initiated), he should put himself in the position of a voyeur and make his own interpretation of a spectacle, even though he ignored an essential element.

Yet this «dismountable likeness» was not Duchamp's ultimate achievement. At the age of eighty, he gave further proof of his «meta-irony» by beginning, in December 1967, a series of nine engravings on the subject of lovers. Inspired by Cranach, Ingres, Courbet and Rodin, he imitated them with mischievous pastiches (see p. 71); or, utilizing publicity photographs, he executed *After Love, The Incandescent Burner, One More Bride Stripped Bare* and *King and Queen,* which were variations of his own themes. To the end he attacked pedantry and exaggerated self-importance, and protested against making art a religion to such an extent that one was precluded from joking about a picture, even one of his own, as if that were a sacrilege.

His last evening, Tuesday October 1st, 1968, he spent in his studio in Neuilly, where he had invited Man Ray and his wife Juliet to dinner, as well as Robert Lebel, who has related what took place. Duchamp reported that he had been obliged to make a trip to listen to a lecture on himself and that he had not understood a single word, because he was seated *too near* the speaker. His guests were thus subtly given to understand: people must stand off a way to judge him properly. He leafed through a recent volume of Alphonse Allais. «These are premortem works,» he declared; «the posthumous works will follow, *but who will publish the others?*» Consistently, even at the end, he defended his conviction that what an artist did not do was just as important as what he did. Dinner over, he went to bed, fell asleep, and his heart stopped beating at five minutes after one in the morning; he died as phlegmatically as he had lived. This American by adoption, who had remained the most typically Norman of any citizen in the world, was buried next to his family in Rouen, and on his grave was inscribed the epitaph he had selected: «Besides, it is always the others who die.» In February 1969 his «dismountable likeness» was shipped to the Philadelphia Museum, where it took three months to reassemble it and where it was unveiled on July 7th without fanfare, as he had wanted.

The smile of Marcel Duchamp speaks now to posterity and dares us to imagine, on the basis of the pictures he has left us, what a Postimpressionist, Cubist, Futurist, Surrealist, Kinetic painter he would have been if he had only been willing to follow a single path and to produce works in a single genre. This smiling revolutionary, who delighted in plays on words and objects, achieved much more than a style; he substituted the concept of a work of being for the concept of a work of art. For him, painting was not *doing* but *being*; and that included all that he did not do because of his negative principles, even though he was quite capable of doing it. Duchamp's motto, which went beyond the «What do I know?» of Montaigne, is inscribed on a note on his *Green Box*: «Perhaps nothing.» Where one believes there may be something, perhaps there is nothing; and where one believes that there is nothing, there may be everything. *Nothing* and *perhaps* bear a constant relationship to each other in society; Duchamp, expressing this verity through his paintings and the objects he made, forced both artists and the public to question the tastes of the day and to put art on a higher level than art had previously occupied.

Valise, 1941–42 and 1952   Contains reproductions in miniature of the works of Marcel Duchamp,
16½″ × 14⅞″ × 4⅜″   Collection: Lydia and Harris Lewis Winston (Dr. and Mrs. Barnett Malbin), New York

BIOGRAPHY

1887 Marcel Duchamp was born on July 28 in Blainville (Seine-Maritime). His father, Justin-Isidore, known as Eugène Duchamp, was a notary; his mother was the daughter of the painter Emile Nicolle. He had two older brothers: Gaston (born in 1875) and Raymond (in 1876); and was to have three younger sisters: Suzanne (in 1889), Yvonne (in 1895) and Magdeleine (1898).

1902 While a student at the Bossuet School in Rouen, he began to paint.

1904–1905 After a first trip to Paris to visit his brother Gaston (alias Jacques Villon), he completed one year of military service in Rouen and in Eu.

1906 In October, he returned to Paris to live on the Hill in Montmartre. Began to do caricatures for the *French Courier* and *Laugh*.

1908 He settled in Neuilly, 9 Avenue Amiral-Joinville, where he stayed until 1913.

1909 For the first time exhibited two pictures at the Salon of Independents (one a view of Saint-Cloud which was sold for 100 francs) and three pictures at the Autumn Salon. Participated in the Exhibition of Modern Painting of the Norman Society in Rouen and designed a poster for it.

1910 Became a member of the Puteaux Group, initiated by his brothers Jacques Villon and Raymond Duchamp-Villon. Beginning of his friendship with Francis Picabia. Showed four paintings at the Salon of Independents and five at the Autumn Salon, of which he became a full member.

1911 Exhibited *The Bush* and two landscapes at the Salon of Independents, *Sonata* at the Modern Painting show of the Norman Society, *Dulcinea* and *Young Man and Girl in Spring* at the Autumn Salon. The last painting was a wedding present for his sister Suzanne, who married a pharmacist she divorced soon afterward. Illustrated Jules Laforgue's poems. The Coffee Mill was his first «mechanical painting.»

1912 His *Nude Descending a Staircase* was rejected for the cubist section of the Salon of Independents, but was shown at the cubist exhibition of the Dalmau Gallery in Barcelona. In May, attended a performance of *Impressions of Africa* by Raymond Roussel at the Antoine Theatre. Spent two months (July and August) in Munich, where he painted *Bride* and *Passage from the Virgin to the Bride,* renouncing the use of a brush. Took part in the Salon of the Section of Gold (from October 10 to October 30).

1913 At the Armory Show in New York (February 17–March 15), a huge exhibition of modern art which assembled almost 1300 works (among them the finest creations of Matisse, Picasso, Kandinsky, etc.), his *Nude Descending a Staircase* caused a sensation which put them all in the shade. Duchamp left Neuilly for a studio at 23 rue Saint-Hippolyte in Paris. He accepted a position at the Sainte-Geneviève Library. Apollinaire mentioned him in *Cubist Painters.*

1915 During the war he was exempt from military service because of a heart condition and decided to voyage to the United States. He arrived in New York on June 15 and received a hero's welcome; according to H.-P. Roché, next to Napoleon and Sarah Bernhardt, he was the best-known Frenchman in America. A first interview in *Arts and Decoration* in September. Sponsored by Louise and Walter Arensberg, he met through them a whole group of nonconformist artists, among them Man Ray, who would become one of his closest associates. Invented readymades.

1916 In April, the Montross Gallery of New York had a showing by the «Four Musketeers,» Duchamp, Jean Crotti, Gleizes and Metzinger. Was a founding member of the Society of Independent Artists and became friendly with Katherine S. Dreier.

1917 Resigned from the Society of Independents, which had refused to show his urinal, *Fountain.* Founded two periodicals with H.-P. Roché: *The Blind Man* and *Rongwrong.*

1918 Painted his last painting in oil: «*Tu m'*». Journeyed to Buenos Aires, where he created a series of chess pawns and executed his picture on glass: *To Be Looked at (from the other Side of the Glass) with One Eye, Close to, for Almost an Hour.* Death of Raymond Duchamp-Villon.

1919 Stay in France from July to December, during which he made his readymade, *L.H.O.O.Q.* (a retouched reproduction of the Joconda).

1920 Back in New York in January, worked with Man Ray on his first optical machine. Birth of Rose Sélavy, whose portrait is a photograph of Duchamp masquerading as a woman. Founding of the Corporation, of which he would be secretary for many years.

1921 Published *New York Dada* with Man Ray, and in June sent the telegram: «Pode bal» to the Dada Salon in Paris. Passed the summer and the fall in France, frequenting the group of *Literature,* led by André Breton.

1922 Spent the year in New York working to complete his Large Glass, the *Bride Stripped Bare by Her Own Bachelors,* to which he had devoted eight years, numerous notes and preparatory studies.

1923 Returned to Paris in February; rumor had it that he had left his Large Glass unfinished and that he had definitely given up painting. Began his liaison with Mary Reynolds.

1924 Perfected a system to win at roulette at Monte Carlo. Executed his second optical machine, *Rotary Demisphere.* Became chess champion of Haute-Normandie. Appeared in René Clair's *Intermission* and in a skit of *Temporary Closing* on Adam and Eve.

1925 Duchamp's father and mother died a few days apart.

1926 Resumed his optical experiments with *Anemic Cinema,* a film he made in collaboration with Man Ray and Marc Allégret. Rented a studio at 11 rue Larrey, the door of which became famous.

1927 Organized a Brancusi exhibition at the Arts Club of Chicago. On June 7, in Paris, married Lydie Sarazin-Levassor, whom he divorced six months later.

1928–1933 Played in chess tournaments in Paris, Hyères, Marseilles, the Hague, Nice, Prague and Folkestone. Wrote and translated studies on the first and final moves of chess games.

1934 In September, publication of his *Green Box* and start of his surrealist period.

1935 Offered six *Rotoreliefs* at a stand of the Concours Lépine (August 31–October 1).

1936 Participated in surrealist exhibition in London and in «Fantastic Art, Dada and Surrealism» at the Museum of Modern Art in New York.

1937 First one-man show at the Arts Club of Chicago (nine works, catalogue of Julien Levy). Designed the door of the surrealist gallery «Gradiva,» 31 rue de Seine. Wrote the chess column for the newspaper, *Ce Soir.*

1938 As «chief arbitrator,» organized an international exhibition of Surrealism in Paris at the Beaux-Arts Gallery.

1941 Publication of the *Box-in-a-Valise,* containing his complete works.

1942 Returned to United States to settle there permanently. Landed in New York on June 25. Collaborated in periodical *VVV,* put out by Surrealists in exile, and in the exhibition: *First Papers of Surrealism.*

1944 Worked on one episode in Hans Richter's film, *Dreams That Money can Buy.*

1945 Did a cover for the March issue of *View* devoted to him. Did display windows for Brentano's Bookstore in New York.

1947 For the international exhibition of Surrealism at the Maeght Gallery in Paris, he conceived the room of Superstitions, rain curtains and the cover of the catalogue.

1950 Reviewed the artists of the Corporation, whose works were offered to the Yale University Art Gallery.

1952 Exhibition of the «Duchamp brothers and sister» at the Rose Fried Gallery, New York. Film with Hans Richter: *8 × 8.*

1954 Married Alexina Sattler, nicknamed Teeny. The Louise and Walter Arensberg Collection, comprising forty-three works of Duchamp, was placed in the Philadelphia Museum.

1955 Became a naturalized American citizen.

1957 Exhibition of the three Duchamp brothers at the Solomon R. Guggenheim Museum. Lecture on *The Creative Process* at the American Federation of Arts in Houston.

1959 Took up residence at 28 West 10th Street in New York. Member of the College of « Pataphysics » of Paris, its Grand Vizier and Master of the Order of the great « Gidouille. » A guest of honor at the international exhibition of Surrealism at the Daniel Cordier Gallery in Paris.

1960 Elected to the National Institute of Art and Letters in New York.

1961 Degree of Doctor *honoris causa* from Wayne State University in Detroit, Michigan. Delivered a lecture on his work at the Detroit Institute of Arts.

1963 Death of Jacques Villon and of Suzanne Duchamp. First large retrospective show at the Pasadena Art Museum, from October 8 to November 3 (114 works).

1964 *Homage to Marcel Duchamp* at the Schwarz Gallery in Milan, which reproduced thirteen readymades in multiples of eight.

1965 During the summer, in Cadaqués, executed nine engravings of the details of the Large Glass for Arturo Schwarz.

1966 Completed and signed *Given 1) the waterfall, 2) illuminating gas,* an environmental construction on which he had been working secretely since 1946. Went to London for an important retrospective show at the Tate Gallery (June 18–July 31).

1967 Started nine engravings on the subject of Lovers.

1968 On February 5, took part in John Cage's *Reunion* in Toronto, and on March 10 in *Walkaround Time,* a ballet of Merce Cunningham, at the University of Buffalo, New York. Died in Neuilly on October 2.

BIBLIOGRAPHY

WRITINGS BY MARCEL DUCHAMP

Liard. Box of 1914, made in 3 copies.

L'Opposition et les cases conjuguées sont réconciliées, in collaboration with V. Halberstadt (Edition de l'Echiquier, Paris and Brussels, 1932).

La Marisée mise à nu par ses célibataires, même. Green Box (Paris, Editions Rrose Sélavy, 1934).

Rrose Sélavy (Paris, G.L.M., 1939).

Marchand du Sel. Ecrits réunis et présentés par Michel Sanouillet (Paris, le Terrain vague, 1958).

A l'Infinitif. White Box (New York, Cordier and Ekstrom, 1967).

Duchamp du Signe. Nouvelle édition revue et augmentée des écrits, établie par Michel Sanouillet et Elmer Peterson (Paris, Flammarion, 1975).

WORKS ABOUT MARCEL DUCHAMP

PIERRE CABANNE: *Entretiens avec Marcel Duchamp* (Paris, Pierre Belfond, 1967).

ROBERT LEBEL: *Sur Marcel Duchamp* (Paris, Trianon Press, 1959).

CALVIN TOMKINS: *The World of Marcel Duchamp* (New York, Time Inc., 1966; French translation by Jacques Papy: *Duchamp et son Temps* (Paris, Editions Time-Life, 1973).

ARTURO SCHWARZ: *The Complete Works of Marcel Duchamp* (New York, Harry N. Abrams, Inc. 1970 and revised edition).

JEAN SUQUET: *Miroir de la Mariée* (Paris, Flammarion, 1974).

PIERRE CABANNE: *Les Trois Duchamp* (Paris, la Bibliothèque des Arts, 1975).

JEAN CLAIR: *Marcel Duchamp ou le grand Fictif* (Paris, Editions Galilée 1975).

PHOTOGRAPHS

Lee Boltus, Milan – Enrico Cattaneo, Milan – Geoffrey Clements, New York – E. Dulière, Brussels – Maison Ellebé, Rouen – John Evans, Ottawa – Jacqueline Hyde, Paris – Paul Katz, New York – Joseph Klima, Detroit – Robert Mates, New York – James Mathews, New York – Otto E. Nelson, New York – Joseph Szaszfai, New Haven – Alfred J. Wyatt, Philadelphia.

We should like to thank the owners of the works of Marcel Duchamp which are reproduced in this volume.

MUSEUMS

National Library, Paris – Peggy Guggenheim Foundation, Venice – Solomon R. Guggenheim Museum, New York – Nordrhein Art Collection Westfalen, Düsseldorf – National Museum of Modern Art, Paris – Rouen Museum – Museum of Modern Art, New York – National Gallery of Canada, Ottawa – Philadelphia Museum of Art – Seattle Art Museum – Yale University Art Gallery.

GALLERIES

Cordier & Ekstrom, Inc., New York – Xavier Fourcade, Inc., New York.

PRIVATE COLLECTIONS

Madame Marcel Duchamp, Villiers-sous-Grez – Dieter and Miriam Keller, Stuttgart – Dr. and Mrs. Barnett Malbin, New York – Mary Sisler, United States – Vera and Arturo Schwarz, Milan.

ILLUSTRATIONS